THE CONVENIENT TERRORIST

THE CONVENIENT TERRORIST

Two Whistleblowers' Stories of Torture, Terror, Secret Wars, and CIA Lies

JOSEPH HICKMAN
&
JOHN KIRIAKOU

Hot Books

Hot Books may be purchased in bulk at special discounts for sales
promotion, corporate gifts, fund-raising, or educational purposes. Special
editions can also be created to specifications. For details, contact the
Special Sales Department, Skyhorse Publishing, 307 West 36th Street,
11th Floor, New York, NY 10018 or info@skyhorsepublishing.com.

Hot Books® and Skyhorse Publishing® are registered trademarks of
Skyhorse Publishing, Inc.®, a Delaware corporation.

Visit our website at www.hotbookspress.com

10 9 8 7 6 5 4 3 2 1

Library of Congress Cataloging-in-Publication Data is available on file.

Cover design by Brian Peterson

Print ISBN: 978-1-5107-1162-4
Ebook ISBN: 978-1-5107-1164-8

Printed in the United States of America.

Table of Contents

Cast of Characters

ABU ZUBAYDAH—A SAUDI ARABIAN CITIZEN AND TORTURE VICTIM, CURRENTLY BEING DETAINED AT THE GUANTANAMO BAY DETENTION FACILITY

JOHN KIRIAKOU—A FORMER CIA AGENT; NOW WORKING AS A COUNTERTERRORISM CONSULTANT

"AMIR"—AN ARAB-AMERICAN CIA OFFICER WHO WORKED SUPPORTING JOHN KIRIAKOU IN PAKISTAN

MAJOR KHALID—A PAKISTANI MILITARY OFFICIAL WHO WORKED WITH CIA OPERATIVES IN PAKISTAN

MOHAMMED SHAM—BOYHOOD FRIEND OF ABU ZUBAYDAH

"AMIN"—UNIVERSITY FRIEND OF ABU ZUBAYDAH

KHALID SHEIK MOHAMMED (KSM)—A MILITANT OFTEN CREDITED AS THE CHIEF ARCHITECT OF THE 9/11 ATTACKS, CURRENTLY BEING DETAINED AT THE GUANTANAMO BAY DETENTION FACILITY

OSAMA BIN LADEN—FOUNDER OF AL QAEDA, EXECUTED BY US SPECIAL FORCES IN 2011.

ABDUL RASUL SAYYAF—LEADER OF THE ISLAMIC UNION FOR THE LIBERATION OF AFGHANISTAN, CURRENTLY A MEMBER OF PARLIAMENT IN AFGHANISTAN

PRINCE TURKI AL-FAISAL BIN ABDUL AZIZ—SAUDI INTELLIGENCE CHIEF

KALIL AL-DEEK—ASSOCIATE OF ABU ZUBAYDAH INVOLVED IN PLANNING "MILLENNIUM ATTACKS"

IBN AL-SHAYKH AL LIBI—FRIEND OF ABU ZUBAYDAH

BRUCE JESSEN AND JAMES MITCHELL—TWO PSYCHOLOGISTS WHO DEVELOPED THE TORTURE PROGRAM EMPLOYED BY THE CIA AFTER THE 9/11 ATTACKS

ALI SOUFAN—FBI AGENT INVOLVED IN THE QUESTIONING OF ABU ZUBAYDAH

MAHER—RELATIVE OF ABU ZUBAYDAH

Author's Note

On December 9, 2014, I waited in front of my computer for the Senate Select Intelligence Committee to release a report on torture. The report had not yet been made public, and I was very anxious to see what it would say. I believed one of the people who would be featured in the 499-page report was a high-value detainee being held in Guantanamo named Abu Zubaydah.

When the report was finally made public, I found that I had been correct. Abu Zubaydah was mentioned. However, there was also something surprising in the report. Something I had not been expecting at all. Namely, that Abu Zubaydah was mentioned more than one thousand times.

Reading this report was personal for me. In fact, it was probably the most personal thing I'd ever read. Eight years earlier, I had been in the military and assigned to an intelligence unit at Guantanamo Bay. In this capacity, I had participated in that operation that had transferred Abu Zubaydah from CIA custody into custody of the Department of Defense. Years later, I was hired as the lead researcher on the Abu Zubaydah *habeas* defense team. I worked on that team for two years, and in those two years I threw myself completely into the details of Abu Zubaydah's life—learning everything there was of his biography, analyzing government documents concerning him, and interviewing his family, friends, and associates. Through this research, the one thing I became absolutely certain of was that Abu Zubaydah was *not* the number three man in the Al Qaeda organization— as the US government had proclaimed at the moment of his capture (and as many in the government still claim to this day). To the contrary, there was compelling evidence that Abu Zubaydah was *not even a member* of Al Qaeda. Yet it also became bracingly clear that he was not an innocent dupe or naïve fellow traveler, as many civil rights and humanitarian groups had contended.

In the real world, a person's life is complicated. It does not always fit easily into a simple category that explains it entirely—like "terrorist mastermind" or "blameless follower." Abu Zubaydah's life was just that.

It *is* just that.

Abu Zubaydah is a real person—not a terrorist monster and not, for lack of better words, an innocent lamb. While the US government and Abu Zubaydah's attorneys continue to go back and forth—as they do to this day—there remains one thing upon which both sides agree. And that's that neither side wants the complete, muddy truth about Abu Zubaydah to come out. Sometimes the truth hurts everyone, and serves nobody's agenda. Unfortunately for him, Abu Zubaydah is the perfect example of such a case.

John Kiriakou is good friend of mine and a former CIA officer—one of the agents who had originally captured Abu

Zubaydah in Pakistan in 2002. Years later, he went to prison for having revealed that Abu Zubaydah had been tortured.

When John was released from prison, we reconnected because we knew we had a story to tell. About Abu Zubaydah and his associates, yes, but also about something more. We knew that together we had information about torture and the pursuit of terrorists by the US government that had never been made public. And that would change everything.

We knew that we had to tell this story.

Joseph Hickman, 2017

Introduction

By David Talbot

Recently the *New York Times* made a bid to expand its editorial spectrum by hiring a columnist outside the newspaper's neoliberal mold. Did the newspaper hire a philosophical soul mate of Bernie Sanders, the most popular politician in the country? Did it choose a rising African-American essayist or a voice of America's threatened immigrant or Muslim communities? Or, a passionate critic of the country's war-addicted national security state? No, the *Times* poached neoconservative Bret Stephens from the *Wall Street Journal*—a climate change denier, unrepentant apologist for the disastrous US invasion of Iraq, and anti-Muslim bigot. During a plague season of fake news and presidential mendacity on a level never before seen, the newspaper of record brought on board a spin artist known for his crackpot science and imperial mania. This is what counts as intellectual diversity in the establishment media.

Hot Books seeks to break this corporate mold with a bold catalog that includes urgent works of investigative journalism, searing memoirs, and political jeremiads. The imprint debuted with D. Watkins's powerful essay collection, *The Beast Side: Living (and Dying) While Black in America*, and continued to challenge conventional wisdom with books like *American Nuremberg*, Rebecca Gordon's war crimes argument against our country's top political and military leaders, and *Unspeakable*, my own extended conversation with fearless journalist Chris Hedges about America's most taboo topics. More recently, Hot Books has published *Horsemen of the Apocalypse* by Dick Russell and Robert F. Kennedy Jr., about the corporate energy titans at the heart of the Donald Trump presidency who are responsible for the end of the world as we know it.

And in your hands, you hold *The Convenient Terrorist* by Joseph Hickman and John Kiriakou, two whistle-blowers who defied the awesome power of the US national security colossus to tell their fellow Americans the truth about the endless war on terror. As Hickman and Kiriakou write here, this war has plunged the country into a "weird wonderland" where truth is a fiction, allies become enemies, and vice versa, and the greatest threats to America are often generated by those in charge of protecting us.

Hickman, a US Army and Marine veteran who blew the whistle on the abuse of prisoners at the Guantanamo Bay prison complex, and Kiriakou, a CIA veteran who served time in prison for exposing the agency's use of torture, are uniquely qualified to tell the sordid epic of Abu Zubaydah, the "convenient terrorist" whom the United States exploited to justify its own reign of terror in the Middle East. They bring an intimate knowledge to this labyrinthine world that cannot be found in the flood of gung ho, jihadi-busting Hollywood propaganda films and embedded journalism about US imperial adventures.

Other new Hot Books coming out in 2017 include Mark Schapiro's *Seeds of Resistance*, about the grassroots movement to challenge the corporate stranglehold on the elements of life; *Without a Country: The Untold Story of America's Deported Veterans* by J. Malcolm Garcia; *The Watchdogs Didn't Bark: How the NSA Failed to Protect America from the 9/11 Attacks* by Ray Nowosielski and John Duffy; and *Inside Job: How American Elections Are Still Rigged Against Voters* by Steven Rosenfeld.

Throughout the country, there is a growing resentment against elites who "know better." They don't. They get it wrong all the time—about wars and weapons of mass destruction, about assassinations of our leaders, about food and drug safety, and about looming financial and environmental disasters.

We're sick of being bamboozled and flimflammed. It's time for us to seek second opinions, to find more credible sources of information. The truth is disturbing. And we need to be disturbed.

The truth is hot, and it's in your hands. Read on.

David Talbot, May 2017

Foreword

By Jason Leopold

Six months after the September 11, 2001 terrorist attacks, the United States captured its first so-called "high-value terrorist." A thirty-year-old Saudi national of Palestinian descent named Zain Abidin Mohammed Husain, better known as Abu Zubaydah.

Abu Zubaydah is arguably one of the most important jihadists to have emerged in the nearly two-decade long Global War on Terror. He has a cameo in the infamous August 6, 2001 Presidential Daily Brief, warning President George W. Bush that Osama bin Laden was determined to attack the United States.

Most notoriously, perhaps, Abu Zubaydah, was the guinea pig for the CIA's torture program and was the first detainee subjected to the drowning technique known as waterboarding.

After his capture, top Bush administration officials asserted that Abu Zubaydah was the "third or fourth man in

Al Qaeda," had served as a "senior lieutenant" to bin Laden, "managed a network of training camps," and had been "involved in every major terrorist operation carried out by Al Qaeda."

But as this extraordinary book by former Guantanamo guard Joseph Hickman and veteran CIA officer John Kiriakou—the man who lead the team that captured Abu Zubaydah—lays bare, the Bush administration's narrative was, at best, highly exaggerated or, at worst, an elaborate lie.

Years later, Department of Justice attorneys working for the Obama administration, quietly recanted nearly every major claim the Bush administration had leveled against Abu Zubaydah, explaining that the government's understanding of his role in Al Qaeda's terrorist-related activities "has evolved with further investigation." Remarkably, the Justice Department admitted that Abu Zubaydah was never even a formal member of Al Qaeda.

Yet despite these revelations, Abu Zubaydah remains a mystery. His story, from young computer engineering student to mujahedeen fighting the communists in Afghanistan to "high-value" detainee housed in a secret facility at Guantanamo Bay, is largely unknown.

Thankfully, the publication of *The Convenient Terrorist* ensures that the Abu Zubaydah's account gets a real public airing. At the same time, the book provides readers with deep insights into the jihadi mind-set at a time when average young men and women across the globe were joining the Islamic State and launching attacks.

But more importantly, this milestone of a book raises new questions about the capture and detention of Abu Zubaydah. Is it possible the United States has been holding the wrong man captive for all of these years? The years long investigation by Hickman and Kiriakou, based on numerous interviews and never-before-seen government documents, deepens the mystery.

I have interviewed Hickman and Kiriakou more than a half-dozen times over the past ten years, and I have come to know both men personally. Their shared passion for speaking truth to power and their fearlessness in holding powerful officials accountable for misdeeds are the embodiment of patriotism.

The pairing of Hickman, the former Guantanamo guard who was on duty when Abu Zubaydah was rendered to the prison in 2006, with Kiriakou, the accused terrorist's captor, is brilliant. Both men are important figures in their own right, whistle-blowers who have paid a hefty price for publicly revealing government abuse in the Global War on Terror. For Hickman, it was the scandalous "suicides" that took place at Guantanamo in 2006, which was the basis for his first book *Murder at Camp Delta*. By revealing the truth about the death of the detainees, he was vilified by high-ranking military and government officials. And Kiriakou is the only person who was prosecuted for "crimes" related to the Bush administration's torture program. His so-called criminal act? Disclosing details about the torture program and that Abu Zubaydah had been tortured. For that, he was sentenced to more than two years in a federal penitentiary.

Hickman and Kiriakou, however, get the last word in *The Convenient Terrorist*. It will surely ruffle feathers when the Deep State gets its hands on it.

Jason Leopold, March 2017
Los Angeles, California

Chapter One

Takedown

The CIA had been looking for Abu Zubaydah for a long time.

Yet for a person occupying the upper echelons of its list of most-wanted terrorists, he remained mysterious. The Agency knew very little about his particulars. Perhaps the only thing they were sure of was that Abu Zubaydah was the third highest-ranking man in Al Qaeda, the infamous international terrorist organization that had slaughtered more than 3,000 American citizens only a few months before. In the CIA's hasty list-making that had followed, Zubaydah was ranked only behind Al Qaeda deputy leader Ayman al-Zawahiri and Osama bin Laden himself.

By late February 2002—after several delays and missteps—the CIA was finally hot on Abu Zubaydah's trail. And John Kiriakou was there.

Kiriakou had arrived in Pakistan only a month earlier as the CIA's chief of counterterrorism operations. The work was hard and the hours were brutal, and not just for him. It

1

wasn't unusual for all employees in the CIA's Pakistan office to work sixteen- or eighteen-hour days, six or seven days a week. The Pakistani weekend is Friday and Saturday. On a normal week, a CIA operative in-country might allow himself the luxury of sleeping in until 8:00 a.m. on a Saturday before going to the office to start yet another day. Kiriakou was enjoying this rare additional snooze time when his phone rang. It was the senior CIA officer in Pakistan. All he said was: "John, get in here as soon as you can. Something very important has come up."

By the time Kiriakou arrived at the office, the chief had already convened a meeting. The chief's deputy, a collection of CIA officers and FBI agents, and the chief himself sat around a large conference room table.

"Abu Zubaydah is somewhere in Pakistan," the chief announced. "The number three guy. And it's our job to catch him."

Headquarters had sent a cable to the CIA office in Islamabad several hours prior, announcing that Abu Zubaydah's presence in the area had been confirmed. However, when you really got down to the details, they didn't have much more. It turned out that—beyond this single cable—there wasn't anything to go on. The intelligence from HQ indicated that he could be in Faisalabad—Pakistan's third-largest city with a population of over four million—but there was also reason to believe he could also be in in nearby Lahore, or in Peshawar (where he had previously run a safe house for Al Qaeda operatives), or even in Karachi, the second-largest city *in the world* and a place where Al Qaeda fighters had been successfully "blending into the crowd" for years.

And that was precisely the problem. Pakistan is the size of Texas and has two-thirds the population of the United States. To just say, "He's in Pakistan. Find him" demands something almost impossible. The CIA team in-country had little manpower, an unspecified budget, and—despite this—a deadline of yesterday. In an attempt to be supportive, CIA Headquarters had cabled the office in Islamabad daily with "leads" that were meant to be helpful, but often provided conflicting or useless information. They did little more than waste the agents' time.

With only a small group of CIA officers, Kiriakou was tasked with both sifting through these Headquarters leads and developing independent ones. His early efforts had proved utterly useless, and involved guesses so off-base they turned out to be almost comical. One memorable instance had involved a wild goose chase that ended in a raid on a local police station, and another had found him investigating a maternity hospital. However, as the CIA would later learn, Abu Zubaydah's movements during this period were purposeful. He was indeed hiding. He was very aware that the United States was looking for him. If Kiriakou had been feeling around for a needle in a haystack, it was because that was exactly what Abu Zubaydah wanted him to do.

Excerpts from Abu Zubaydah's own diary, later recovered by the CIA, reveal a wariness during this time.

"February 8, 2002: I am now in Lahore since two days ago. We are now in a temporary house with the Pakistani brothers."[1]

"February 9, 2002: News came from Karachi that the Pakistani Police raided one of the houses which had a number of our brothers in it, and it arrested 20 brothers. Two hours later, a group of Americans came and photographed the location, or they photographed themselves with their weapons, at the location, like Rambo."[2]

"February 10, 2002: We moved to another house, or more precisely, two houses, and divided ourselves in it. This is also temporary. And in order to arrange our matters and split from our Pakistani brothers, rather the Arabs, too, in another house, completely independent and isolated. We will stay this way, unsettled. We cannot start any (new) program."[3]

"February 10, 2002: The Pakistani newspapers are saying that I am in Peshawar, trying to reorganize Al Qaeda, for war against the Americans."[4]

Only once did the small CIA team in-country come close to Abu Zubaydah, and only after patrolling the streets of Pakistan's major cities all night long for an entire week. The device they'd used—the details of which remain classified— had picked up Abu Zubaydah's trail in Faisalabad, but for only a few seconds. Rushing to his location, the CIA had, alas, found nothing. He had slipped away once more, and his trackers had no idea where to go next. A blip and he was gone.

But still, a blip.

After this initial period of struggle and frustration—with missives from Headquarters continuing to come in (and continuing to be completely useless)—Kiriakou asked the CIA's Counterterrorism Center for help. He received a top CIA targeting officer, who arrived in Islamabad a few days later and immediately began poring over the thousands of pieces of data the Agency had amassed relating to Abu Zubaydah as his constantly changing location.

This "targeteer"—as the agent was known—began by taping a huge roll of paper—the size of a small American-style billboard—to the wall of a CIA conference room, and putting Abu Zubaydah's name in the center. From that, like spokes of a wheel, were radiated out the names of people known to be associated with Abu Zubaydah, their addresses, and all other identifying data that had been collected. Every time something new was uncovered, up it went on the board. After a week or two, the thing looked like a strange work of postmodern art—a spider's web of data that pointed to fourteen specific sites, each one a potential location for Abu Zubaydah (and possibly for his cohorts).[5]

They began to formulate a plan for hitting these sites. The first obstacle was that the CIA had never before carried out more than two raids in a single night in Pakistan. Fourteen simultaneous raids would be unprecedented, and would require a much larger team. Still, Kiriakou knew that it was the approach that offered the best chance of success. It was what needed to be done. So he made his pitch.

Kiriakou began by requesting that Headquarters provide a team of several dozen agents—half CIA and half FBI—along with weapons, communications gear, night vision equipment, battering rams, and other tools of the trade. He also asked for a budget of several million dollars for "incidentals," including safe houses, rental cars, food, water, and hotels to house this new and expanded team.[6]

Because of Abu Zubaydah's prominence and priority, Kiriakou got what he wanted, and quickly. Langley chartered a plane, and forty-eight hours later an expanded team arrived with new manpower, money, and equipment. They set up a base in a local hotel, renting out an entire floor. Because of the sheer size and scope of what was happening, maintaining a low profile was impossible. In addition to the DO NOT DISTURB signs placed on every door on the entire floor, the sight of men who were obviously Americans bringing dolly-loads of crates containing electronic equipment, weapons, and ammunition raised the eyebrows of the hotel's

Pakistani security guards. The guards demanded to see what the crates contained. A fistfight nearly broke out between one of the local guards and a newly arrived CIA officer. The tension was only dispelled when Kiriakou arrived on the scene and told the guard that the hotel manager, a British national, had approved of all the equipment.[7] Of course, no such approval had been given. However that, and the discreet passage of 100 rupees to each guard, nipped further problems in the bud.

As soon as the joint team was fully ensconced in the hotel, Kiriakou and an Arab-American CIA officer called Amir set out to find private houses in both Lahore and Faisalabad that would be suitable for setting up more secure field operations. Both officers had a working acquaintance with Lahore, and had already been in the city for several weeks. They also maintained a liaison relationship with the relevant Pakistani military authorities assigned to work on the case. Major Khalid, a Pakistani military official who had been assigned to show them the town, recommended a neighborhood popular with retired senior military officers. The houses in this neighborhood were huge and the properties spacious. Such homes would provide the privacy that would be necessary both for operations and for when the targets were captured.

The house they finally selected was enormous—it had nearly a dozen bedrooms, which would be perfect for initial interrogations. It was also isolated. Another plus. Pakistani cities generally have no street signs, which can make it hard to know where you are at any given time. When one gives or receives directions, they are usually something along the lines of, "Make a left at the Pepsi billboard. Make a right at the orphanage. Go straight past the vegetable market, then bear left at the shoe store." The Lahore safe house was not only isolated, it was down a web of unmarked streets with very few landmarks. Finding it would be a challenge. Which was exactly what the team wanted. But it was also immediately a problem.

After renting the place fully furnished, Kiriakou and Amir went back to the hotel to begin transferring the equipment to the new digs. They had rented a couple of large passenger vans and believed that three trips between the hotel and safe house ought to do the trick. They headed back to the hotel just as the sun set, but no sooner had they loaded the vans then realized that they couldn't recall how to get back to the safe house, especially in the dark.

Kiriakou was able to remember that when he'd come out of the front door of the house for the first time, he'd seen a McDonald's restaurant in the distance. Thus, he suggested to Amir that they go to the McDonald's near the hotel—a different McDonald's—and ask for directions. Once there, they ordered some food and asked how to get to the McDonald's in the safe house neighborhood. The employees either didn't speak English or had no idea where any other McDonald's happened to be. Kiriakou[8] asked to speak to the manager. Did *he* know where the other McDonald's might be? The manager looked at Kiriakou with a blank stare. He was from Multan, not Lahore, he said, and could barely make his way from his own apartment to the McDonald's where he worked. He did think he could help, though. He handed Kiriakou a placemat that went with kids' meals. It had cartoon characters on it, but also showed, very generally, the locations of other McDonald's restaurants in the city. He handed it over with a smile and Kiriakou gladly accepted it, realizing that—for the time, at least—it might be the only way back to the safe house. After two more hours of driving around the unnamed streets of that city of so many millions, using a fast food placemat as a map, they found it. In another hour, they had backtracked to the hotel and carefully documented every step of the way. Kiriakou resolved that there would be no getting lost again.[9]

Faisalabad was next. Neither Kiriakou nor Amir had ever been to Faisalabad before. In fact, neither had even heard of the city until arriving in Pakistan, despite the fact that it had nine million residents. The two drove to Faisalabad while the rest of the team remained at the hotel. As before, the first order of business would be to buy or rent a house from which to launch the raids, house the officers and equipment, and, eventually, do initial interrogations once they had prisoners in custody.

Faisalabad was a dark and rough place. Most structures seemed to be made of hardened mud or cheap concrete block. Not a single building in the city was more than ten stories. And the city was utterly impoverished. Kiriakou had the impression the entire place smelled of rotting garbage. Children swam in open sewers along the sides of the dirt roads. People traveled in overcrowded buses, on scooters, in trucks, on donkeys, rickshaws, or camels. It seemed they would hop onto anything that moved.

This time, Kiriakou and Amir went with the easy route. They hired a real estate agent who took them to a half dozen large, mostly upper-class homes around the city until they finally found a suitable place located along a putrid canal. The stench was overpowering, but the house was big enough to handle everything the team would need.[10]

Once a winner had been selected, still accompanied by the real estate agent, Kiriakou and Amir walked up to the roof terrace and checked their GPS units to see how many satellites they were able to catch and how strong the cell phone signals were.

Smiling, Kiriakou turned to the real estate agent and said, "We'll take it. Will you accept cash?"

Taken aback, the real estate agent stammered, "Sir, do you mind if I ask you a question? What do you do for a living?"

Kiriakou had been too exhausted to formulate a cover story for use with civilians. He stood there with a blank look on his face until Amir jumped in.

"We're textile barons," Amir said. "We bought a textile factory just outside of town."

The realtor lit up.

"Wonderful, sir! Wonderful! Faisalabad is the Birmingham of Pakistan. So many Pakistanis work in textiles. Thank you for bringing jobs to our country!"

Kiriakou was relieved this had worked, and made a promise to himself to get a story straight before going out again.

Another issue with which Kiriakou and Amir had to deal was the fact that CIA Headquarters had not authorized them to disclose the target's name to Pakistani intelligence. This was because the CIA believed that the Pakistanis were likely to either leak the information to the press or, worse, intentionally tip off Al Qaeda or Abu Zubaydah himself and foil the operation. Thus, CIA officers opted to refer to Abu Zubaydah only as "the big fish," which later became "Mr. Fish." The CIA leadership in-country thought this was ridiculous. The Pakistanis, after all, were willing to shed blood in the operation, and had time and again proven their willingness to help. Kiriakou thought it was downright disrespectful for the CIA to ask them to put their lives on the line, and then turn around and tell them they weren't trustworthy enough to know the identity of the target.

So with the senior officer's support, Kiriakou and Amir decided to go against policy and tell their Pakistani counterpart, Major Khalid, and his top officers that it was Abu Zubaydah in the crosshairs. The Pakistanis kept the secret.[11]

The day before the raids, Kiriakou, Amir, and Major Khalid decided to personally drive by each one of the fourteen target sites to assess safety. Questions needed to be answered. Was there easy ingress and egress at each site? Were there any indicators that it could be a setup? Were there adequate escape routes in case the raid fell apart? Were the streets wide enough to get the necessary vehicles through? Was there a risk of crossfire?

Most of the targets were going to be located in one- or two-room mud huts with thatched or corrugated tin roofs. One location turned out to be a shish kabob stand with a payphone. The team scratched that site off the target list. (Obviously, there were Al Qaeda fighters hiding in the neighborhood and using the payphone for their communications, but little could be done. They could not raid all the surrounding blocks.)

In the middle of this review of the sites, Kiriakou's cell phone rang. It was the targeting officer calling from Islamabad. A "friendly intelligence service" had called, he said.

"They got a walk-in this morning who said that a big group of Arabs from Afghanistan was hiding in a big, brightly painted house in Faisalabad,"[12] the officer said.

A walk-in was a person who literally just walked into a foreign Embassy and said he had intelligence he to pass along (usually in exchange for money).

Kiriakou asked if the team could talk directly to the walk-in.

"No, they refuse to do that," the officer said. "No face-to-face."

Kiriakou wondered aloud if the "walk-in" might actually be a telephone intercept. Why would a supposedly friendly intelligence service deny the CIA access to a source? It didn't make sense.

One way or the other, Kiriakou knew his team was basically still on its own. Now they were just on their own while also on the lookout for a brightly painted house.[13]

Then, an hour later—still on patrol and having just passed through the campus of the University of Faisalabad—the group saw it. It was one of their targets—a huge house with a bright, fresh coat of paint.

One of Khalid's men was the first to speak.

"I can tell you right now that there are bad things going on in that house," he said. "Look. It's the only house in the neighborhood with all the shutters closed. Nobody keeps their windows like that."

Kiriakou saw that this was indeed correct. It was the middle of the day and almost 100 degrees. It had to be sweltering inside. Even so, someone had decided to keep the windows closed up tight.

"We're going to need a bigger team on that one," was all Kiriakou said.[14]

Leaving the enormous, colorful house behind, they headed onward to the final site left on their tour. The team had placed this site on the list because Abu Zubaydah's contacts had referred to it offhand several times in intercepted communications. The problem was that the address the team had turned out to be a vacant lot.

"How can this be?" Kiriakou asked when they arrived, seeing the kabob stand all over again. "We were certain about this address."

"No, no, this is common," Major Khalid's security officer responded.

He explained that in large Pakistani cities, each plot of land was assigned a unique telephone number. The nearest telephone pole would be wired for the number. But what frequently happened was that someone would climb the pole, splice the wire, and run the wire to his house. This would allow the interloper to make as many calls as he or she liked, and the bill will go to the owner of the vacant land.

"This happens in Pakistan all the time," the security officer said.[15]

He then asked a young Pakistani technical officer to climb the pole. The tech did so, and began sorting through the Medusa's head of wires. Eventually, he found the one he was looking for. As Kiriakou looked on, the tech followed the wire literally hand-over-hand down the pole and then down an alley. Finally the tech stopped, pointed at a nondescript middle-class house in the distance, and said: "It's that one."[16]

Kiriakou and Amir looked at each other and smiled. Kiriakou spoke first.

"We got him."

At that point, the two split from the group of Pakistanis and went back to the hotel for a couple hours of sleep.

It would be days before anybody would sleep again.

Around 7:00 that evening, Kiriakou and Amir left the hotel for the safe house and the final briefing.

As they approached their passenger van, Amir turned and said, "So what do you think is going to happen tonight? Do you think we'll get him?"

Kiriakou honestly didn't know.

"By this time tomorrow, we'll either be heroes or our careers will be over," he said.[17]

From Abu Zubaydah's diary:

"March 20, 2002: I do not know whether I informed you. We have left Lahore (my group and I, after a brief separation). We met in Faisalabad, in a suitable big house, but it does not lack security gaps. The brothers who arranged it for

us fell in it, but no problem, as long as the house is temporary.
I am still trying to find the suitable person (as a cover), and
then determine the suitable location. The house (will be) in
the suitable city to stay for the winter. So that I can arrange
our special programs."[18]

Around 10:00 p.m., Kiriakou stood on a coffee table in the
Lahore safe house surrounded by dozens of CIA officers, FBI
agents, and Pakistani military officers. He looked at his men
confidently, smiled, and set the tone by saying: "At the risk
of sounding like something from a movie . . . the first thing
we're going to have to do is synchronize our watches."

The plan was this: At 11:00 p.m., two rented buses would
leave for Faisalabad carrying several dozen team members,
including their Arabic translators. A small group would remain behind in Lahore. Then, at precisely 1:30 a.m., all teams
would leave the safe houses and travel to the target neighbor-
hoods.

Kiriakou explained: "At 1:50 you get out of the car and
get into place. At 1:55, have eyes on the target. At 2:00 you
break down the door."[19]

Kiriakou repeated the standard operating procedure.
Break down the door with battering rams. The Pakistanis go
first, the FBI goes in second, and the CIA third.

The Pakistanis were there to secure each room and separate the men from the women and children. Men would
be handcuffed, while women and children would either
be moved to another room or, if the house was small, outside. The FBI would tag each room and search for evidence.
(The September 11 attacks were still an open criminal investigation.) The CIA would then take custody of any males
captured. These males would then be transferred to the safe
houses for an initial joint CIA/FBI interrogation.[20]

Kiriakou and Amir saw the groups off, one team to each target site, then went to the roof of the Faisalabad safe house. It then became a waiting game. At 2:00 a.m., Kiriakou looked at his watch and said to Amir, "Oh-two hundred. Here we go."

Seconds later, Kiriakou and Amir heard a sound—distant but not too distant. It was the dull *"boink, boink, boink"* of metal on metal. They exchanged a glance.

The noise was coming from a location they had been calling Site X.

"That's the Abu Zubaydah site," Amir said. "It has to be."

Kiriakou picked up a walkie-talkie.

"Base to Site X, come in."

No response. Kiriakou pulled out his cell phone and called the Site X team leader.

"What's going on out there?"

He learned that the door had been reinforced with steel, and the team couldn't break it down. And then came the sound of gunshots.[21]

"We've got to go there," Kiriakou barked to Amir.

The two ran to their rental car and sped to Site X, only a few minutes away down the empty streets. When they arrived, the scene was chaos. People were running and screaming, and Pakistani security officers were trying to get control of things. Outside the house lay one man who was clearly dead; another near him was unconscious and looked near death. A third was covered in blood and screaming.[22]

Kiriakou grabbed the senior Pakistani at the site.

"Where is Abu Zubaydah?"

"*This* is Abu Zubaydah," he said, pointing to the man who was down and unconscious.

He had been shot in the thigh, groin, and stomach with an AK-47. Amir was excited.

"We got him!" he cried.

Kiriakou wasn't so sure. The man looked nothing like the six-year-old passport photo of Abu Zubaydah that the CIA had been using. That photo showed a thin, handsome young man with a closely cropped beard and moustache. The man lying bloody on the ground was forty pounds heavier, clean shaven, and had long, wild hair.[23]

Kiriakou called Islamabad to ask what to do.

"Get me a picture of his iris," the targeteer said.

Kiriakou shouted in Arabic at Abu Zubaydah. "Iftah ayounak!" Open your eyes. But Abu Zubaydah's eyes had rolled back into his head. Taking a picture of them might be physically impossible. Kiriakou told the targeteer as much.

"Okay, then get me a close-up of his ear," the targeteer said. "No two people on Earth have the same ears. They're like fingerprints."

Kiriakou carefully photographed the man's ear, plugged the camera into his phone, downloaded the image, and sent it to Islamabad. A minute later, the targeteer called back.

"It's him."[24]

Some hours afterwards, the story of what had transpired became clear. The house had been full of Al Qaeda fighters, mostly young ones. They'd been on the first floor. A locked door had separated them from three more people upstairs—Abu Zubaydah, his bodyguard, and a Syrian bomb maker. The younger men downstairs didn't even know who was on the second floor. Abu Zubaydah and his friends ate alone, never came downstairs, and never spoke with anybody else in the house. A Pakistani "tea boy" brought food every day and left it outside their door.[25]

By the time the CIA team had been able to get through to the second floor, the three men inside had climbed to the roof and had tried to jump to the roof of the neighboring house to escape. They had left behind a treasure trove of intelligence, including Abu Zubaydah's diaries and a partially constructed bomb—the soldering iron still hot—along with the plans to the British school in Lahore on the table.[26]

The Syrian bomb maker had jumped first. He was shot and killed instantly by team members below, dying even before he hit the ground. Abu Zubaydah jumped next and nearly met a similar fate. The bodyguard jumped last. He took an AK-47 shot to the center of his femur, shattering his leg.[27]

But Abu Zubaydah was the priority. After ascertaining his identity, Kiriakou, Amir, and two Pakistanis lifted him and threw him in the back of a filthy Toyota pickup truck that the Pakistanis had commandeered and sped to the nearest hospital. By then it was 2:30 a.m.[28]

The hospital was the worst Kiriakou had ever seen. All its windows and doors were wide open. Swarms of mosquitos fed on the open sores and wounds of its patients. In places, cats and dogs wandered the halls. The floors were slick with both grime and bodily fluids. The beasts fed on it.[29]

At one point, Kiriakou saw medical personnel trying to keep hypodermic needles sterile by jamming them into a bar of Irish Spring soap. When somebody needed a shot, a nurse or doctor would remove one of the needles, rinse it off with unpotable tap water, fill the syringe, and administer the injection. The physician would then rinse the needle off again and jam it back into the bar of soap.[30]

The medical staff, of course, were not expecting an international emergency in the middle of the night. What they got was more than a dozen people, half of whom were obviously Americans dressed as Pakistanis wearing bulletproof vests, and two severely wounded Arabs.

Abu Zubaydah was bleeding to death. Kiriakou grabbed one of the doctors by the collar and said, "This man is very important. You have to save his life. And you have to do it quickly."

The doctor was stunned. He just stood there, speechless.

Kiriakou shouted, "Let's go! He's bleeding to death."

The physician seemed to understand. A makeshift trauma team wheeled Abu Zubaydah and the bodyguard into adjacent operating rooms.

While this was happening, word of what had just transpired was spreading across the Al Qaeda community. Kiriakou knew that in about an hour, braver members of Al Qaeda were likely to start driving past the hospital and firing shots at the building.

Kiriakou explained his concerns to Major Khalid.

"If they realize we're so lightly armed, we're all dead," he concluded. "Any chance you can get a helicopter here?"

Khalid said he could.

Satisfied, Kiriakou stepped into the operating room. "Doc! Wrap it up. We have to get out of here."[31]

Khalid made good on his word. Thirty minutes later, a Pakistani Army helicopter touched down in the hospital parking lot. It was nearly 5:00 a.m., and the city was waking up around them. The CIA team loaded Abu Zubaydah—patched up and bleeding a little less—along with his wounded bodyguard onto the chopper. Kiriakou, Amir, Khalid, and a young CIA case officer got on after them. They flew directly to the closest military base that had a hospital wing.[32]

There was no chaos at the military base. The Pakistanis knew the team was coming and were prepared for the gravity of Abu Zubaydah's injuries. Even so, not long after the team arrived, the lead doctor pulled Kiriakou aside and informed him, "I've never seen injuries so severe where the patient lived. It'll take a miracle to save him."

Abu Zubaydah was given large quantities of blood, much of which ended up soaking his sheets and pooling beneath him. He was full of so many holes that the physicians could not seem to keep them closed. To Kiriakou, the scene was like something out of the 1950s. Though a step up from the filthy city hospital, the equipment in the military hospital was still dated, blood and fluids were dispensed from glass bottles, and the gurney looked like it had come out of an episode of *Marcus Welby, MD*.

As the physicians continued to work frantically on Abu Zubaydah, Kiriakou's cell phone rang. It was the targeteer in Islamabad.

"Headquarters says 24/7 CIA eyes on. Don't leave his side."

Kiriakou slumped into a chair. He had already been awake for nearly twenty-four hours, and now he had to make sure Abu Zubaydah didn't go anywhere. After the doctors got him stabilized, Kiriakou tore a sheet into strips and tied Abu Zubaydah's wrists and ankles to the bed.

"What are you doing?" asked one of the physicians.

"No offense, doc," said Kiriakou, "but I don't know you or your staff. My orders are that this man doesn't go anywhere. And I'm going to make sure he doesn't."[33]

The sun rose. Kiriakou turned the ceiling fan to its highest setting to blow away the mosquitos. He sat the foot of Abu Zubaydah's bed and tried to stay awake. Abu Zubaydah was comatose and still. Alive, but just barely.

Mid-morning, Kiriakou phoned Amir.

"Do you mind bringing me a change of clothes from the safe house? I need a pair of underwear, a shirt, and a pair of socks."

An hour later, Amir materialized with clothing, a couple of packages of crackers, and a small container of orange juice. By chance, he had brought Kiriakou's special T-shirt—something he only wore for sleeping, a gift from his children. It was bright red, with a large yellow SpongeBob Square Pants in the center. Kiriakou looked at it and smiled.[34]

A couple of hours later, Abu Zubaydah began to stir. Kiriakou stood at the foot of the man's bed, hands on his hips, watching the prisoner come to. Abu Zubaydah opened his eyes and focused squarely on SpongeBob. It was the moment when he realized something along the lines of, "Oh, my God . . . the Americans have me."

His heart rate soared from 120 to nearly 200 in just a few seconds. The machines to which he was attached began beeping loudly and a trauma team raced into the room. He looked as though he might die.[35]

"He's going into ventricular fibrillation," the doctor said. The medical staff shocked Abu Zubaydah with a defibrillator, and his heart rate slowed to 110. A dose of Demerol went into his IV, and then Abu Zubaydah was unconscious again.[36]

It was four hours before Abu Zubaydah began to stir once more. Kiriakou, still trying to keep himself awake, noticed the man's fresh movements. Kiriakou got up and stood at the foot of the bed. Abu Zubaydah opened his eyes and fixed a stare right at him. Then he motioned with his tied right hand for Kiriakou to come closer. Kiriakou walked over to the side of the bed. He moved Abu Zubaydah's oxygen mask to the side, leaned over, and asked in Arabic, "What is your name?"

Abu Zubaydah just shook his head.

Kiriakou repeated the question. "What is your name?"

Abu Zubaydah responded in English.

"I will not speak to you in God's language."

"That's OK, Abu Zubaydah," Kiriakou said. "We know who you are."[37]

Abu Zubaydah began to drift and rave, sometimes bizarrely.

"Give me a glass of red wine," he called at one point.

Kiriakou exchanged a glance with a nearby physician.

"Did he just ask for a glass of red wine?" Kiriakou asked.

"He's hallucinating," the doctor responded. He pumped another shot of Demerol into the IV and Abu Zubaydah was out again. Kiriakou settled back into his chair and continued to wait.[38]

Several more hours passed, and Abu Zubaydah awoke in what was now clearly terrible pain. He frantically motioned with his tied hand for Kiriakou to approach. Once more, Kiriakou moved the oxygen mask aside.

"What can I do for you?"

As he spoke these words, Kiriakou realized that Abu Zubaydah was crying.

"Please, brother. Kill me. Take the pillow and kill me."

Even despite the man's grievous wounds, Kiriakou was not expecting this request.

"No, my friend. Nobody's going to kill you. We worked hard to find you, and we have a lot of questions we want to ask you."[39]

Abu Zubaydah began crying loudly.

"Please kill me!"

Kiriakou responded angrily.

"You got yourself into this mess," he said. "Fifty thousand people worked in those towers. What did you think was going to happen? Did you think we wouldn't come after you?"

Abu Zubaydah turned away in his bed. He was weeping quietly now.[40]

"I didn't want to attack America. I wanted to kill Jews."

Kiriakou ignored the remark and its absurd implications.

"I'm going to give you some advice," Kiriakou said. "I'm the nicest person you're going to meet in this entire experience. My colleagues aren't as nice as I am. Your life is at a crossroads. The rest of it can be relatively easy, or it can be terrible. That'll be up to you. Whatever you do, I urge you to cooperate."[41]

Abu Zubaydah turned back toward Kiriakou.

"You seem like a nice man. But you're the enemy. I'll never cooperate. Besides . . . I'm going to die."

"On the contrary," Kiriakou told him. "You're going to get the best medical care the United States has to offer. You're going to get the best doctors in the world."[42]

Kiriakou's words were proved true. A few hours later, the targeteer called. A private jet was on its way. CIA Director George Tenet had asked a top trauma surgeon from Johns Hopkins University Hospital to fly from Baltimore to Pakistan. He would lead Abu Zubaydah's medical team and accompany the patient to an "onward location." It would be a few hours until the plane touched down.[43]

As they waited for the American surgeon, Abu Zubaydah became equal parts garrulous and nervous. He told Kiriakou that he had many regrets in his life. He would never know "the touch of a woman," he said, or "the joy of fatherhood." He was upset at the prospect of being taken out of Pakistan. "What's going to happen to me?" he repeated again and again. At several junctures, he asked Kiriakou if he would be killed.

"Just relax," Kiriakou told him. "There will be a doctor onboard and he'll take care of you. Nobody's going to kill you."[44]

Finally, the surgeon arrived. The hospital unit was situated alongside the taxiway, so the plane was able to land within a few hundred feet of it. Abu Zubaydah was numb from stress and another dose of Demerol. He asked Kiriakou to hold his hand as Kiriakou and three FBI agents carried the gurney to which he was strapped out to the tarmac. They lifted him upright to get him through the plane's door and carried him to the back of the aircraft. A few minutes later, Abu Zubaydah was gone, receiving the attentions of a surgeon somewhere high in the sky.

Five days after the raid, on April 2, 2002, White House Press Secretary Ari Fleischer made an announcement to a room full of reporters.

"Abu Zubaydah was arrested by Pakistani police, and will be handed over to US authorities," and went on to say Abu Zubaydah's capture "represents a very serious blow to Al Qaeda."

The story was picked up by all major media outlets. It wasn't Osama bin Laden, but Americans would take it. From coast to coast, the capture of Abu Zubaydah was hailed and applauded.

Many took to blogs and social media to make it clear they advocated swift justice for what this man had done to America. But as years went by, it became obvious swift justice was not in the cards. For the next four and a half years, Abu Zubaydah was moved from country to country and placed in a series of secret makeshift prison camps operated by the CIA. His whereabouts at any given time were known only to a few top members of the Bush administration and handpicked members of the CIA. For the rest of the world, it was as if he disappeared off the face of the earth.

During this period, the people who followed Abu Zubaydah's story in the news began to notice a puzzling trend. The government officials, who had once so harshly condemned him and called for his capture, began to speak about him using different tones. He was no longer a top terrorist mastermind, and certainly not the number three person in the Al Qaeda organization. In fact, officials stopped mentioning him in connection to Al Qaeda entirely. And, likewise, to the 9/11 attacks. Instead, those in the know began referring to him only as a "high-value detainee" who had information about the Al Qaeda organization.

On September 6, 2006, Abu Zubaydah was taken out of CIA custody and sent to Guantanamo Bay, Cuba, where—as of the time of this writing—he is still in custody. This person—upon whom the US government spent millions of dollars to find, capture, and airlift from a foreign country—has now been held in custody for fifteen years without being charged with a crime.

Obviously, this raises many questions. Why did the US government change its attitude about Abu Zubaydah and his connection to Al Qaeda? Is he a terrorist? If so, why has he not been charged with a crime? If not, why has he been in custody for a decade and a half?

Some believe the government does not want Abu Zubaydah to go to trial because it would be revealed in the hearing that he was tortured while he was in CIA custody. This, however, turns out to be a distraction. While the government may not want further details of torture programs to become public, there is more at stake.

To understand the real reason why powerful entities do not want Abu Zubaydah's full story to come out, you have to undertake a close examination of his biography, his friends, and his associates. When you do that, you begin to realize you are looking at something nobody was ever meant to see.

Chapter Two

Born Without a Country

Zayn al-Abidin Muhammad Husayn—the man later known as Abu Zubaydah—was born in Riyadh, Saudi Arabia, on March 12, 1971. His parents had migrated there from the West Bank of Palestine five years before. His father worked as a schoolteacher in Riyadh, and his mother was a homemaker. From his earliest moments, Abu Zubaydah understood that he was in a unique situation. Even though his parents lived in Saudi Arabia, they were not citizens. Because of that, under Saudi law, neither was he.

Abu Zubaydah had nine brothers and sisters. The family was middle class. His mother and father were, generally, loving parents who tried to do what was best for their children. His parents would often travel to the West Bank, and take their children with them so they could visit with their grandparents, uncles, and aunts who still lived there.

According to interviews with Abu Zubaydah's family members, he was a normal child who enjoyed the typical games and activities. However, Abu Zubaydah was notably different in at least one important way. He was highly intelligent, as his family quickly realized. He liked to read newspapers and books. He listened to western music, and would dance to 80s pop records. He consumed every kind of culture he could find.

At the age of ten, he started questioning the status quo in Saudi Arabia. He did not think the citizenship rules were fair. He thought the way immigrants around his neighborhood were treated by Saudi citizens was unjust. (In Saudi Arabia—then as now—immigrants were often resented, ostensibly for taking jobs away from Saudi citizens.)

By the time Abu Zubaydah reached his teens, he'd found a handful of likeminded friends to hang out with. They would listen to Western music and watch American movies together. They particularly liked Michael Jackson. Abu Zubaydah's closest friend, Mohammed Sham, recalled the day he and Abu Zubaydah had visited every record shop in Riyadh on a quest to find a music video of Michael Jackson's hit "Billie Jean." When they finally located a copy, the two watched the video over and over until they had memorized the singer's dance moves precisely.

Sham and Abu Zubaydah would also often drive around the neighborhood in Sham's father's car, discussing religion and politics. One night, the topic turned to Palestine. While both of the youths agreed that Palestine should be a separate state from Israel, they disagreed about how best to accomplish this. Sham believed separate statehood should be accomplished through negotiations with Israel. Abu Zubaydah thought it should be achieved through Jihad. Abu Zubaydah felt this was justifiable according to the Koran, and that Allah would assure the Palestinians' victory. The discussion got so heated that it devolved into a fight. And after that night, Abu Zubaydah never spoke to Sham again.

After Abu Zubaydah stopped talking to his best friend, his attitudes became more extreme. He announced that he was for an all-out rebellion against the Saudi society. This caused a great deal of stress in his home. Abu Zubaydah's father wanted him to embrace the Saudi culture as his brothers and sisters had done—to dress like a Saudi and follow the traditions and customs to which Saudi citizens adhered. Abu Zubaydah refused, and typically dressed in Western clothes. His typical uniform was jeans and a T-shirt. For most of his teens, Abu Zubaydah remained a sullen loner without any real friends.

As he prepared to graduate from high school, Abu Zubaydah felt he had no country to truly call home. He decided he would go to college in India, to the University of Mysore, and study computer science. More than anything, his motivation was to get as far away as possible from what he considered a "despicable country."

Abu Zubaydah's father did not want him to go to India. He wanted Abu Zubaydah to instead attend college somewhere in Saudi Arabia. Yet as his son became more and more insistent, his father eventually relented—giving his blessing and even agreeing to pay for Abu Zubaydah's education abroad.

India turned out to be a great disappointment. Abu Zubaydah arrived expecting to find a welcome respite from the culture that had made him feel denigrated and oppressed for so many years. Instead, he found entirely new things to perturb him.

The city of Mysore was a melting pot of Muslim and Hindu cultures. Abu Zubaydah found the Hindu religion to be both silly and sinful, and quickly decided that he despised its beliefs. He found the Muslims in the city to be "lukewarm" and half-hearted in their adherence to the faith. From what

Abu Zubaydah could see, they seemed to have surrendered to the influence of Hindu culture.

Abu Zubaydah was once more unhappy. Once more, he felt as though his culture was being repressed and stifled. In addition, he was now truly alone, with no parents or siblings to support him. When he was not attending classes, he spent almost all of his time alone in the room he rented from a Muslim family. There he would study, read, and write poetry.

One day in the campus courtyard, he chanced to meet another Muslim student named Amin. Amin was a devout Muslim. He was also—like Abu Zubaydah—a foreign student, having been born and raised in Kuwait. Amin and Abu Zubaydah instantly became very close friends. It turned out that Amin embraced the same ideology that Abu Zubaydah had concerning Islam, and they were in agreement on most political issues concerning the Middle East—especially those concerning Palestinians.

Abu Zubaydah learned that Amin was planning to go on a trip to Afghanistan to receive Jihadi training. At the time, Afghanistan was in the middle of a civil war. Just two years earlier, the Mujahedeen had defeated the Russian army. Now the Mujahedeen was mopping up Afghanistan's Soviet-backed government, which was still in power. Though the country was nominally under control of this communist-backed government, a large portion of it was now actually ruled by the Mujahedeen.

During the war against the Soviets, several Mujahedeen groups had created military training camps throughout the areas they occupied. These camps were funded and supplied by nations like the United States and Saudi Arabia, and offered free military training not only to Mujahedeen fighters combating the Soviets, but to all Muslim men across the world. During the 1980s and 1990s, tens of thousands of men traveled to these camps to receive training in military skills. Most of these men would not fight against the Soviets. Rather, their mission was simply to learn skills that they could call upon if necessary in their home countries. The vast majority returned directly to their normal lives after receiving their training, and never engaged in combat.

Amin soon convinced Abu Zubaydah to accompany him on an adventure to Afghanistan to receive Jihadi training. On January 13, 1991, they began the journey, taking a train from Mysore, India to Peshawar, Pakistan. There, they stayed at a guest house operated by a Mujahedeen group called the Islamic Union. The guest house was code-named "The House of Martyrs." It was one of three Islamic Unity guest houses in Pakistan. The other two were known as "The House of Supporters" and "The House of Conquerors." Virtually all petitioners seeking Jihadi training in Afghanistan training camps came through Mujahedeen-operated guest houses like this.

Abu Zubaydah and Amin quickly became acquainted with other Muslim men making the same journey. They also learned they would be undergoing their training in a facility known as Khaldan Training Camp. They were told that once their training had been completed, they would be conducted safely back to Pakistan. That was—if they chose to come back. They learned they would have the option—if they so chose— to stay in Afghanistan and fight alongside the Mujahedeen against the communist-run Afghan government forces.

A week after Abu Zubaydah and Amin had first arrived at the guest house, they boarded a pickup truck that took them across the Pakistani border into Afghanistan. The ride became brutal. The mountainous terrain was dangerous, and the roads were in poor condition. To kill time, Abu Zubaydah got to know the other passengers in the vehicle. There were five in addition to Abu Zubaydah and Amin, and all were from Palestine. Two of these were college graduates who had received their degrees in the United States.

After forty-eight hours of travel, they arrived at Khaldan Training Camp. It was a large facility with many trainees, and Abu Zubaydah found himself greeted by men from all over the world. All of them seemed there for a purpose, but many—including Abu Zubaydah—were not sure precisely what that purpose was.

In the month that followed, Abu Zubaydah's group of trainees learned how to fire AK-47 assault rifles, how to throw grenades, and other basic combat training. Alongside the military tactics, religious training was also dispensed. Abu Zubaydah and his classmates would sit for hours listening to Mujahedeen religious leaders give their takes on Islam, the universe, and what it meant to be a Muslim.

Abu Zubaydah found that he loved both the military and religious training. He also excelled at both. Studying the art of war was fascinating, and he had never felt closer to God. He also enjoyed the camaraderie that quickly formed between classmates. For the first time in his life, Abu Zubaydah was not an outsider or a second-class citizen. Here, he felt as if he truly belonged.

And so, after his training was completed, Abu Zubaydah left the camp and returned to India, but only for a short time. Within a month, he would travel to Afghanistan a second time to fight alongside his new brothers against the communist-backed government. He felt he had finally found a home.

Thus, Abu Zubaydah became what is known as a Jihadist, or a Mujahedeen fighter.

Chapter Three

The True Meaning of Jihad

To understand Abu Zubaydah's life as a Jihadist, it is important to understand what Jihad meant to Abu Zubaydah.

The practice of Jihad has been part of Muslim culture for over 500 years. The Arabic word "Jihad" essentially means "struggle." Accordingly, there are three specific areas of struggle in a Muslim's life and society where they may encounter Jihad. These are:

- Internal Jihad–An individual Muslim's internal struggle to live the Muslim faith and follow the Koran.
- Social Jihad—The struggle to build a good Muslim society.
- Holy War or Military Jihad—The struggle to defend Islam against any real or perceived enemy of the Muslim faith.

A person involved in military Jihad is called a Mujahid. A group of Muslims involved in military Jihad is called Mujahedeen. Military Jihad can be broken down further into two subsets—offensive Jihad and defensive Jihad. These two strains are distinct, and differ greatly in their underlying philosophies.

A report published in 2006 by the Hudson Group, titled "Jihad Ideology in Light of Contemporary Fatwas," defines offensive Jihad as *"a collective duty of the community of Muslims to pursue the infidels into their own lands, to call upon them to accept Islam and to fight them if they do not accept Islam."* In this sense, offensive Jihad is not found in the Koran and for that reason, most Muslim scholars do not believe it is a legitimate form of military Jihad. However, many terrorists and terrorist groups, including Al Qaeda and ISIS, believe deeply in the philosophy of offensive military Jihad.

The same report by the Hudson Group defines defensive Jihad as *"an individual duty for all Muslims to defend Muslim lands when the infidels prepare to attack them or when they attack and occupy them."* This language has a basis in the Koran and is accepted by most Muslim scholars as the legitimate form of military Jihad.

There was not a better example of defensive Jihad in modern history than that of the Afghanistan War. In the late 1970s through the 1980s, as the Soviets invaded, the native people organized and rose up an army of Jihadist, Mujahedeen fighters to defend their homeland, and they received strong support from US, which sent hundreds of millions of dollars—along with weapons—to help them fight the Soviet invaders. Eventually, after ten years of war, the Soviet invaders were forced out.

In the instance of the Afghanistan War, the US government had wholeheartedly and explicitly supported a Jihadi cause. Yet the tenor of the world changed on September 11, 2001. Since that date, the word "Jihad" has been considered as exclusively meaning "offensive Jihad." In many cases, its true meaning has simply become "terrorism."

Since Abu Zubaydah's capture, he has adamantly denied being the number two person under Osama bin Laden—which he was originally accused of being. He has also denied being a member of Al Qaeda and/or practicing their offensive Jihadi philosophy. He has tried to make the case that, instead, the Jihad that he practiced was "defensive Jihad."

He is on record as arguing this in a Combatant Tribunal Review Tribunal Hearing (CTR) at Guantanamo Bay:

> *"Our doctrine was not the same as what USAMA BIN LADEN and al Qaida were promoting, which was and is a doctrine of offensive Jihad."*

In the same review, it became clear that either the Air Force Colonel in charge of the hearing did not believe or *did not understand* the significance of what Abu Zubaydah was saying.

The colonel stated:

> *"What role, offensive or defensive, the individual had in the force is not relevant. Only the fact that the person was a part of the enemy force is relevant...the Tribunal does not take into account the individual's personal beliefs."*

Ironically, while in this instance the US government refused to take Abu Zubaydah's statement into consideration, to this day it has not offered any proof that Abu Zubaydah was ever a member of Al Qaeda. Few would dispute that nations and religious sects have the right to defend themselves when attacked. The Middle East has been invaded, occupied, and often exploited by outside forces for many years, and the line between terrorism and legitimate popular resistance is often less than clear—but this is a fact that a senior military officer should know.

The fact that the nuances involved in Abu Zubaydah's claim were so readily ignored is troubling.

Was it merely an atypical lapse in judgment on the part of the government? Or was it, perhaps, the sign of something infinitely more intentional and sinister?

Chapter Four

Life as a Jihadist

After leaving India and returning to Afghanistan in March of 1991, Abu Zubaydah committed himself completely to his new life as a Jihadist, joining up with a Mujahedeen group known as the Islamic Union. Over the next ten years, he and his new brothers-in-arms would wage war on the communist-controlled Afghan government, as well as on other groups they believed threatened "true Islam."

During the first year, Abu Zubaydah fought in many small battles. He believed that each one was a small step in the greater effort to liberate the Afghanistan people from communist oppression. Abu Zubaydah did not relish the horrors of war. He prayed desperately for victory, but also for peace. His faith in Allah grew.

Between 1991 and 1992, Abu Zubaydah also visited other training camps operated by Mujahedeen groups. In these camps, he received more advanced military training. One such camp was called Al-Forouq. It was operated by a little-known group calling itself Al Qaeda. The Islamic Union had undertaken several joint missions with Al Qaeda in the 1980s and early 1990s, but it was still an unfamiliar outfit for many. Abu Zubaydah would stay with these "Al Qaeda" for three weeks and receive weapons training. It is very likely that during this initial visit he was also introduced to Osama bin Laden.

In December of 1992, Abu Zubaydah received a serious head injury from mortar fire during a battle against Afghanistan government forces. He was taken from the battlefield to a hospital in Peshawar, Pakistan. It took several surgeries and a little over a year for him to recover. During that time, Abu Zubaydah's family in Saudi Arabia received word of his injuries from other Mujahedeen fighters who had served with him. The family sent Abu Zubaydah's older brother Maher to visit him in Pakistan. Maher pled with him to give up his Jihad and come home. Abu Zubaydah refused his brother's request. After his recovery, Abu Zubaydah went to work at the Khaldan Camp as an instructor. Most of his duties were light. He observed trainees firing weapons, and fed new recruits their meals.

Abu Zubaydah quickly became unhappy in the role of trainer and low-level administrator. He wanted greater responsibility and a more active role, but the leadership believed he was not ready. In the summer of 1993, however, Abu Zubaydah finally got his wish to be a part of something larger. He was ordered to the Al Qaeda-run Farouq Training Camp. There, he was given a new mission to train Tajikistani rebels and—alongside them—to conduct military operations. Tajikistan had been under the control of the Soviet government since about 1920. When the Soviet empire began to fall apart, Tajikistan descended almost immediately into a civil war.

It would be in the interest of the United States if the side emerging victorious were to be friendly toward the West. Accordingly, the CIA began to covertly fund Abu Zubaydah's group of rebels, as they appeared the best option for making this happen. Few sources have been made public about the specifics of CIA support in this period. However, Abu Zubaydah's personal diaries confiscated during his capture verify that he was directly involved in training rebels and conducting military operations in Tajikistan with CIA funding. Former FBI Agent Ali Soufan also confirms in his book *The Black Banners* that the CIA was directly funding operations in Tajikistan during this time period. In an article published on July 7, 2009, in *The Rock Creek Free Press*, investigative reporter and former Naval Intelligence Officer Wayne Madsen took it a step further and reported that Abu Zubaydah and his group were receiving funds from the CIA as early as 1991 to combat the Afghani communist regime.

However, it was when Abu Zubaydah conducted the Tajikistan operation that he grew more and more impressed with what he saw of Osama bin Laden, and with the Al Qaeda organization as a whole. Abu Zubaydah was not an official member, and *never became one*. This is, of course, a vital point. Abu Zubaydah did ask if he would ever be able to join, but Al Qaeda leadership told him no, citing concerns arising from his head injury. There is no record of his reaction, though he must have been disappointed.

Meanwhile, the Tajikistan missions continued and were almost uniformly successful. The group specifically trained by Abu Zubaydah enjoyed multiple victories against communist-led factions in Tajikistan.

As the Tajikistan missions concluded, the Islamic Union sent Abu Zubaydah next to Pakistan to oversee logistics for the Khaldan Training Camp. Specifically, he would coordinate travel and lodging for those attending the camp. Again, it is not known how Abu Zubaydah felt about this. Was he ready for a respite from the fighting, or was he disappointed in being given more low-level admin work? However, what *is* known is that during this period, he began to learn how to forge travel documents. Forgeries were often required for camp attendees who had neglected (or tried and failed) to obtain the documents needed to travel between countries. Forgery became a skill Abu Zubaydah would excel at, and something for which he would gain positive notoriety across the entire organization.

In 1995, Pakistan, under immense pressure from the US government, began a program under which suspected Islamic terrorists were hunted and arrested. During one of these new anti-terror sweeps, Abu Zubaydah's house was raided and he was placed in jail for nine months. Pakistan—then as now—remained a country beset by corruption. Consequently, and despite the best efforts of the US, the Islamic Union was often able to bribe local government officials to secure the release of its members. Such was, eventually, the case for Abu Zubaydah. After nine months behind bars, the Islamic Union secured his release, and Abu Zubaydah picked up directly where he had left off. He opened a new safe house under the name "The House of Martyrs" (the same name he had used before), and continued his operations until September 11, 2001.

The CIA became aware of the House of Martyrs safe house, but incorrectly believed it was run directly by Al Qaeda. It was later revealed that Khalid Sheik Mohammed (KSM), mastermind behind the 9/11 attacks, at one point had commanded an Al Qaeda safe house in Kandahar Afghanistan called the "Martyr's House." However, this was different from the House of Martyrs, and the two were not connected. The confusion of the two camps is perhaps understandable in light of the lack of Arabic-speaking intelligence agents within the US government at the time.[45] This error is important because it is likely responsible for the misattribution of a serious allegation against Abu Zubaydah. In the transcripts of the Combatant Status Review Tribunal Hearing for KSM, he states:

> "I was Emir (i.e. commander) of *Beit Al Shudada* (i.e. the Martyr's House) in the state of Kandahar, Afghanistan, which housed the 9/11 hijackers. There I was responsible for their training and readiness for the execution of the 9/11 Operation.[46] (pg. 17-18)"

In his diaries, Abu Zubaydah sets forth that he took over as Emir, or "Prince," of the House of Martyrs in Peshawar, Pakistan in 1994.[47,48] However, he initially mentions the House of Martyrs in January 1991. That specific entry reads,

> "From that office branches many houses for the incoming mujahedeen from outside Afghanistan (Arabs and others). The houses are: Al-Fatiheen [The Conquerors], *Al-Shuhadaa'* [The Martyrs], and Al-Ansar [The Supporters]. The Saudis, Yemenis, Algerians and Palestinians are distributed in these houses. Hani is staying at the House of Martyrs for the mujahedeen from the Great Syria, but there are people staying at the house that are not from the Great Syria."[49]

Abu Zubaydah used the Arabic term "Al-Shudadaa' in his diary entry, while KSM used the Arabic term "Al Shudada" in his testimony at his Tribunal Hearing. Both terms are spelled (and pronounced) identically in Arabic, and both terms mean "martyr." However, there is evidence that "Al-Shudadaa'" and "Al Shudada" have been translated by official government translators differently.[50] Specifically, one translator translated Beit ("house" in Arabic) Al-Shudada as "Martyrs' House" while another translator translated the same to "House of Martyrs."[51]

This is absolutely crucial. There is excellent evidence that US intelligence was confusing a facility run by Abu Zubaydah with one operated by KSM. Abu Zubaydah was the Emir of a House of Martyrs in Pakistan operated by the Islamic Union, while KSM was the Emir of a different Martyrs, House in Afghanistan by Al Qaeda, which was used to train and house some of the 9/11 hijackers. They were not the same. However, the US government's confusion and conflation of the two would haunt Abu Zubaydah for the rest of his life.

In the years directly prior to September 11, 2001, Abu Zubaydah had arranged for hundreds of men to train at the Khaldan Camp. He coordinated the travel for trainees—first from their homelands to a safe house in Pakistan, and then into Afghanistan for training at Khaldan. Though the Khaldan camp was not an Al Qaeda training camp, many Al Qaeda members had trained there, and many of the men that trained at the camp would later become members of Al Qaeda and/or well-known terrorists. One such man was the person notoriously known as the "shoe bomber," Richard Reid. Two others were the 9/11 hijackers Satum Al-Suqami and Majed Moqed.

It's key to remember that during this period Abu Zubaydah was still operating as a conditional ally of the United States. Despite his private opposition to US foreign policy in the Middle East, he was, nonetheless, essentially playing on the same team as the Americans. After the 9/11 attacks, the Islamic Union (still Abu Zubaydah's umbrella organization) joined with the Northern Alliance and agreed to help the invading US forces fight to overthrow the Taliban regime. While Abu Zubaydah was no fan of the Taliban, his diaries clearly show he disliked the US even more. He said that he could not, and never would, support the United States or any country that enabled what he saw as Israeli oppression of Palestine. Abu Zubaydah echoed this sentiment years later when speaking to military interrogators at Guantanamo when he stated:

> *"I am not here to lie to you, or to cheat you, or to lie to myself by saying that I am not an enemy of your injustice. I have been an enemy of yours since I was a child, because of your unjust acts against my people, the Palestinians, through your help and partnership with Israel."*

According to Abu Zubaydah's diaries, a week after 9/11 he left his group and joined a loosely formed band of Jihadists ready to defend Afghanistan against its invaders. His dislike for the Americans was just that strong.

Soon after his new mission began, Abu Zubaydah and his group—and other groups of Jihadist just like them—would witness firsthand the full force of the US military. Within weeks of the invasion's start, their organizations would be destroyed and many of them—including Abu Zubaydah—would be on the run.

It is unclear if, during this time, Abu Zubaydah directly engaged US forces. The US government claims that he did, while Abu Zubaydah and his attorneys adamantly deny it. What is agreed is that, traveling on bombed out roads and through tough terrain, Abu Zubaydah was eventually able to escape into Pakistan. There, in an attempt to disguise himself, he cut his hair short and dyed it. He also shaved off his beard. He stayed at a guest house in Faisalabad that was operated by an Islamic group called Lashkar-e-Tayyiba (LT). LT is an organization that has been labeled by the US government (and many other nations) as a terrorist organization. It has close ties to Al Qaeda.

While at the LT guest house, Abu Zubaydah read local newspapers and surfed the Internet. He would occasionally see his name in reports about the conflict, and learned that a worldwide hunt for him was underway. According to Abu Zubaydah's diaries from this period, this situation confused him. In one entry, he asks explicitly: "Why are they after me? Don't they know I am not Taliban or Al Qaeda?"

As it turned out, Abu Zubaydah would remain at the LT guest house for over a year. Then, on March 28, 2002, the LT house was raided by CIA, FBI, and Pakistani soldiers. Abu Zubaydah was captured, and his new journey as a detainee began.

Chapter Five

The Peshawar Seven

To fully appreciate the situation in which Abu Zubaydah found himself, it's vital to understand the complicated history and shifting alliances involved in the seemingly endless wars in Afghanistan.

When Abu Zubaydah made the decision to enter military Jihadi training in 1991, there were several Mujahedeen groups in Afghanistan happy to offer it. While many Mujahedeen limited their training classes to people living in Afghanistan, there were a few that made themselves open to all Muslim men, regardless of country of origin or residence. The training camps also differed from one another in their underlying Islamic ideology. When Abu Zubaydah and his college friend Amin first made up their minds to undergo training, they had to follow an application process that would route them into one of these open groups that took outsiders. To do this, they contacted an organization called "Maktab al-Khidamat" (MAK), also known as the Afghan Service Bureau. MAK was the forerunner of Al Qaeda's recruiting operation, and was instrumental in creating the fundraising and recruitment network that would benefit Al Qaeda and other warlords and Jihadi groups throughout the 1980s.

During the Soviet-Afghan war, MAK's mission was to raise funds and recruit Mujahedeen fighters from all over the world to stand against the invaders. It received hundreds of millions of dollars from the US and Saudi governments and donations from Muslims charities all around the world. (Approximately thirty million from charities located in the United States.)

MAK was operated by two prominent figures in Afghanistan at the time—Dr. Abdullah Yusuf Azzam and Osama bin Laden. Their fundraising and recruitment efforts supported seven distinct Afghan Mujahedeen parties that fought against the Soviet-installed Democratic Republic of Afghanistan forces. They became known as the Peshawar Seven. This alliance sought to function and present itself as a united diplomatic front, and even sought representation in the United Nations.

The leaders and their groups of the Peshawar Seven alliance were:

Mohammad Yunus Khalis, leading the Khalis faction

Gulbuddin Hekmatyar, leading Hezbi Islami

Burhanuddin Rabbani, leading Jamiat-i-Islami

Abdul Rasul Sayyaf, leading the Islamic Union for the Liberation of Afghanistan

Ahmed Gailan, leading the National Islamic Front for Afghanistan

Sibghatullah Mojaddedi, leading the Afghanistan National Liberation Front

Maulana Mohammad Nabi Mohammadi, leading
Islamic and National Revolution Movement of Afghanistan

While these seven groups were the only ones to directly receive financial and martial support from the US and Saudi governments, they often disbursed what they received to smaller subgroups. One of those smaller subgroups was Osama bin Laden's Al Qaeda.

MAK also maintained a close relationship with Pakistan's Inter-Services Intelligence (ISI) agency, through which the CIA and Al Mukhabarat Al A'amah, the intelligence agency of Saudi Arabia, funneled money and weapons to the Peshawar Seven. One of MAK's core functions was also to arrange and pay for travel for new recruits—first to Pakistan, and then into the Afghan regions for training.

MAK was a sophisticated operation, and maintained silence and security at all turns. It compartmentalized information, ensuring that its workers knew only what they needed to, and nothing more. For example, if a worker's job was to send money to the Mujahedeen, that worker would know nothing about the weapons that would be purchased with the money. It was a simple policy, but ultimately an effective way to protect sensitive information. Many believe that three-letter agencies in the United States had taught it to MAK.

After the Soviet withdrawal in 1989, the United States behaved as if its mission were accomplished. The United States government stopped financially supporting the Mujahedeen, and stopped sending it weapons. Many of the Mujahedeen leaders despised the US for this, and saw it as abandonment just when help was needed the most. The country was in ruins after the war. Almost immediately, an Afghan civil war broke out. And even though the Soviets were gone, the country still essentially operated under a communist system. Amidst this chaos and hardship, the Mujahedeen wanted to make one final, all-important push to overthrow the pro-Soviet government and create a new Islamic government. It was clear the US was not interested in being a part of this. Thus, the Peshawar Seven believed their work was far from over.

The training camps and MAK remained operational, and still received a bit of financial support from Saudi Arabia. The MAK's mission became slightly different, however. The goal was now to train Muslim men in Jihad, and then convince them to fight specifically against the communist Afghan government.

Upon analyzing dozens of Detainee Assessment reports from Guantanamo—and cross-referencing them against Abu Zubaydah's diaries and other FOIA-released documents—it becomes very clear the Islamic Union had four training camps operating during this period: Camps Seda, Bari, Khaldan, and Al-Farouq. Of these, Camp Seda was the largest and most important. It had no trouble finding willing recruits. When Camp Seda was operating at full capacity, Camps Bari and Khaldan often had to take the overflow. From the early 1980s through the early 2000s, tens of thousands of Muslim men trained at these camps.

Praise was lavished on the work the camps were doing by leaders all around the word. Even though explicit US support would eventually be withdrawn, US Presidents Reagan, George H. W. Bush, and Bill Clinton all referred to the operators of these camps as "freedom fighters" and/or "heroes."

It was 1991 when Abu Zubaydah arrived at a training camp run by Abdul Rasul Sayyaf. The Persian Gulf War had just begun. During this period, Sayyaf secretly took on another mission for his group, and that mission would change the world.

Abu Zubaydah decided to commit his life to Jihad, and volunteered to the fight against the communist-controlled government in Afghanistan. Abu Zubaydah aligned himself with Abdul Rasul Sayyaf's group at an important time. It is almost certain that being a new member of the group—a fresh recruit, with no combat experience—Abu Zubaydah was not privy to the group's important operational plans. He probably also was not told how or from where they received funds to train Jihadists and wage war. However, keeping in mind Abu Zubaydah's disdain for the Saudi government, it is also reasonable to think he might have been kept in the dark intentionally. He would have been scandalized and outraged to learn of the agreement Sayyaf had made with the Saudi government, and that the Saudis had become the primary source of money for the Islamic Union. Further, the agreement was new, having commenced only three months prior to Abu Zubaydah's arrival in Afghanistan.

On January 17, 1991, the United States commenced Operation Desert Storm in Iraq. The Iraqi military had invaded Kuwait in August of 1990, and Saudi Arabia was afraid Saddam was not going to stop there. The United States had offered to send troops to Saudi Arabia to guard its borders. The Saudis had heartily accepted. Osama Bin Laden found this arrangement intolerable and sinful. Infidels from the West sending its military to an Islamic country? Disgraceful! And it wasn't just any Muslim country. It was the place where the Prophet Mohammed had been born, and where Mecca was located.

Motivated by his outrage, bin Laden decided to offer up an alternative to the Saudi government, and made his pitch.

He would protect Saudi Arabia from the Iraqi army with his Mujahedeen group Al Qaeda. Just give him the funds and manpower to do it right, and the protection of Saudi Arabia could be an all-Muslim job.

There's evidence the Saudi government considered this option, but most Saudi officials did not believe that Al Qaeda could seriously hope to defend Saudi Arabia from the entire Iraqi Army—at the time, the fourth largest army in the world.

Yet even after being turned down, bin Laden remained strident. He became outspoken on the issue, insisting that it was an obscenity that Americans be allowed to defend Muslim lands. Many Saudis agreed with him. Concerned that bin Laden would foment a political uprising, he was banished from the country by the Saudi government.

Bin Laden returned to Afghanistan as a hunted, marked man. He was forced to live in fear and hiding. He believed the Saudi government would very much like to see him dead, and might have taken steps to make that happen. bin Laden believed Saudi assassins could get to him in Afghanistan with relative ease, so in 1991, bin Laden moved yet again, transporting his entire base of operation to Sudan. Though Abdul Rasul Sayyaf believed bin Laden was ultimately correct in his attitudes, Sayyaf could not openly support bin Laden because Sayyaf's organization was still receiving funds from the Saudis. Yet Sayyaf agreed to continue to train bin Laden's Al Qaeda troops at his camps in Afghanistan. At the same time, the Saudi government's intelligence chief, Prince Turki Al-Faisal bin Abdul Aziz, made a private agreement with bin Laden to pay for the Al Qaeda training. In exchange, the prince received assurances from bin Laden that he would not conduct any terrorist attacks on Saudi soil. Through this agreement, thousands of Al Qaeda fighters were trained.

Some went on to conduct terrorist attacks in Europe and the United States.

This arrangement raises questions and issues that continue to impact political prisoners today. For example, if the United States is holding Abu Zubaydah for war crimes, and accusations against him include the fact that he trained Al Qaeda fighters (including three of the 9/11 hijackers), then why is Sayyaf not also being held? Why isn't his group, the Islamic Union, officially labelled by the US State Department as a terrorist organization?

The answers can probably be found in the role Sayyaf and the Islamic Union played in the twisted history of Afghanistan. Most people in the United States have still never heard of Abdul Rasul Sayyaf. He is rarely mentioned in the media. Despite this, he remains one of the most important and influential people in Afghanistan.

Little is known about Sayyaf's early life. He is reckoned as having been born around 1946. He comes from a town in Afghanistan near the capital of Kabul called Pagman. He is a Pashtun by ethnicity and belongs to the Kharruti tribe. He is a Wahhabi—a member of an ultraconservative sect of Islam that follows the strict rules of Sharia law to the letter. He has a degree in religion from Kabul University, and a master's degree from Al-Azhar University in Cairo.

It was at Al-Azhar, in 1969, that Sayyaf met another Afghan student named Burhanuddin Rabbani. Rabbani was a member of the Muslim Brotherhood—an Egyptian Islamic, political, and social organization. The Muslim Brotherhood was a major influence on the creation of Hamas, and many countries have now labeled the controversial group a terrorist organization.

Rabbani exerted a tremendous influence on Sayyaf, ultimately convincing Sayyaf to join the Muslim Brotherhood.

The two eventually resolved to take this new radical form of Islam back to Afghanistan and start an Afghan chapter.

After completing their studies, Rabbani and Sayyaf both returned to Afghanistan and became professors at Kabul University. There, they pushed their political beliefs on their students and recruited thousands of followers into the Afghan Muslim Brotherhood. Among these recruits was Sayyaf's longtime friend Gulbuddin Hekmatyar—the nation's future prime minister. The Afghan Muslim Brotherhood became known for their extremist beliefs, and for becoming violent with those who seemed to flout the requirements of the faith. For example, it became common practice for members of the Afghan Muslim Brotherhood to throw acid in the faces of unveiled women.

In 1973, Daoud Khan became the leader of Afghanistan. He was a reformer who pushed progressive policies, such as allowing women to work. He also accepted Soviet support for Afghanistan, and seemed close with the Russians. The Afghan Muslim Brotherhood was made furious by this development, and later that same year attempted to assassinate Khan. The attempt failed, and Rabbani, Sayyaf, and Hekmatyar were forced to flee to Pakistan. Media outlets throughout the Middle East and the Soviet Union contended that the assassination attempt had been supported and funded by the CIA. The CIA has never denied the claim.

Three years after the failed assignation attempt, in 1975, Sayyaf decided to risk returning to Afghanistan. He was caught crossing the border and immediately put in prison. Then, three years later on April 27, 1978, President Khan was successfully assassinated by a group of men loyal to Sayyaf. However, the coup by Islamic hardliners, for which Sayyaf had hoped, did not follow. The liberal government was still receiving Soviet support and still too strong to overthrow.

They immediately replaced Khan with a politically similar leader named Nur Mohammed Taraki.

Over the next few months, Sayyaf's followers—along with followers of Rabbani and Hekmatyar—began a military campaign against the government. They pounded the government forces and weakened them considerably. On September 14, 1979, these forces opposing the Afghan government successfully raided the presidential palace. Nur Mohammed Taraki was killed, and the liberal government of Afghanistan was successfully replaced with an ultraconservative government operating under Sharia law. Hafizullah Amin was named leader of this newly formed government. (Many in the Soviet government at the time openly alleged that Amin was a CIA asset.) One of Amin's first acts was to release Sayyaf from prison.

After Amin took office, the communist supporters regrouped and, with the support of the Soviet Union, began to mass weapons and men. Sensing impending doom, Amin reached out to Pakistan and the United States. However, before either nation could respond, on December 27, 1979, KGB agents assassinated Amin at his palace, and within hours, the Soviets had invaded the country.

Sayyaf's old friends Burhanuddin Rabbani and Gulbuddin Hekmatyar—along with other Islamic leaders who had fled to Pakistan during Khan's reign—came back to Afghanistan, and with Sayyaf began recruiting Afghans for Jihad against the Soviets.[52]

The recruitment effort saw direct support from Osama bin Laden, who donated millions of dollars of his own money, and helped create the MAK. Bin Laden funneled money to MAK from the Saudi government and from the United States. The US also permitted MAK representatives free travel in the United States. MAK visited over twenty-one US cities, where its representatives visited mosques and solicited donations and volunteers to fight in Afghan cause. Ostensibly, MAK was recruiting for all of the leaders of the Peshawar Seven, but Sayyaf received the majority of the recruits and money.[53]

By 1982, Sayyaf had a force of nearly 7,000 foreign Jihadist fighters. He had created new training divisions, expanded training camps, and further cemented ties with the United States, Pakistani, and Saudi Arabian governments. He had also begun to take the recruitment efforts worldwide.[54]

During the 1980s, Sayyaf met with many high-ranking political figures from throughout the United States, including President Reagan. Uniformly, these American leaders thanking him for his work fighting the Soviets, and personally pledged their support.[55] Sayyaf continued to receive large amounts of money and weapons from the United States.

In 1988, with victory in sight for the Mujahedeen, bin Laden—with the blessing of Azzam and Sayyaf—created his own organization and named it Al Qaeda (meaning "The Base"). Bin Laden wanted to expand the fight to Islamic causes around the world, especially to Palestine. (It is important to note that all of the original leaders of Al Qaeda were former members of Sayyaf's organization.[56]) An agreement was made between Sayyaf and bin Laden. Sayyaf would train his new recruits in his training camps until bin Laden could create his own training program. In return, Sayyaf would still receive support from MAK.

In 1989, the Soviet army withdrew its troops from Afghanistan, yet the government remained pro-Soviet. In early 1992, when the pro-Soviet backed government fell to the Jihadi groups, Sayyaf's old friend Burhanuddin Rabbani became president. However, Hekmatyar, and a newly-formed group called the Taliban, did not agree with Rabbani's being made president. In the opinion of the Taliban, the man was not adequately conservative. Formerly aligned Jihadi groups began to feud among each other. At the same time, CIA funds—which had ceased after the withdrawal of the Soviets—began once more to flow to Sayyaf. The US said it needed him to train a new Jihadi group in Libya called the Libyan Islamic Fighting Group (LIFG). Originally, that group had been composed primarily of former Libyan Mujahedeen who had fought against the Soviets in the Afghan War. LIGF's goal was to overthrow Libya's President Gaddafi, whom they saw as oppressive and anti-Muslim. With the CIA funds, Sayyaf set up military training bases for the organization in Pakistan. (Ironically, after 9/11, the United States officially labeled LIFG a terrorist organization while still continuing to fund it until Gaddafi was overthrown on October 20, 2011.)

In 1993, Sayyaf took on yet another task, helping to create a Jihadi group in the Philippines called the Abu Sayyaf Group. These Filipino fighters were trained in his training camps in Afghanistan. (Abu Sayyaf Group is officially considered a terrorist organization by the United States.) Between 1992 and 1996, Sayyaf trained thousands of Muslims for Jihad.

In 1996, the Taliban took control of most of the country. Yet Sayyaf, Ahmad Shah Massoud, and a few other less influential warlords still continued battling the Taliban. It is important to note that despite this alliance, Sayyaf and Massoud did not get along. They were polar opposites in religious and political philosophies. Nevertheless, they became partners out of necessity—a perfect illustration of "the enemy of my enemy is my friend."

In 1996, bin Laden returned to Afghanistan from Sudan, and the Taliban welcomed him with open arms. At the same time, the CIA started a top secret operation codenamed "Alec Station." Its mission was to track bin Laden, collect intelligence on him, and run clandestine operations against him and Al Qaeda. The CIA considered using Sayyaf for this, but believed he was too close with bin Laden to ever fully trust. Even so, Sayyaf had been a longtime source for the CIA, so the operators assigned to the mission never reported the connection between Sayyaf and bin Laden, or that Al Qaeda was using Sayyaf's training camps. Instead, the CIA falsely claimed that many of the training camps that had been operated by Sayyaf for years—like the Khaldan, Bari, and Sada training camps—were instead bin Laden's camps. This was verified in an interview conducted with former CIA analyst Marc Sageman, and can be easily confirmed by reviewing DoD detainee assessment reports and military tribunal hearings. The CIA understood the problems that might be created if it became public knowledge that they had been funding Sayyaf since 1973, and that he had facilitated the creation of Al Qaeda.

In December of 1998, bin Laden brokered a meeting between Sayyaf and the Taliban leadership. During this meeting, bin Laden tried to convince Sayyaf to join forces with the Taliban and let bygones be bygones. Sayyaf refused.

The following year, all of Sayyaf's training camps in Afghanistan were raided by the Taliban and shut down. The Taliban then used their influence with Pakistani intelligence (ISI) to shut down all of Sayyaf's training camps in Pakistan as well.

By April of 1999, the entirety of Sayyaf's training camps were closed. Many of his top commanders left the Islamic Union and joined the Taliban. Abu Zubaydah writes about these defecting commanders in his diary, calling them "weak and with no Faith." During this time, despite the many hardships he faced, Abu Zubaydah continued to concentrate his efforts on raising funds for the Islamic Union.

At the very time that the last of Sayyaf's training camps closed, a joint operation between US Special Operations Command and the US Army's Defense Intelligence Agency began. The operation was called "Able Danger." It used data mining techniques to associate open-source information with classified information in an attempt to locate terrorist groups throughout the Middle East, and to make connections among individual members of Al Qaeda. It did not take Able Danger long to find out that Sayyaf was a major figure. Able Danger also identified Al Qaeda cells in the United States that had participated in the 9/11 attacks. One was the "Brooklyn cell" linked to blind Sheik Omar Abdel-Rahman (who had been a classmate of Sayyaf's in Egypt) and the 9/11 attacks leader Mohamed Atta.

In November of 1999, Northern Alliance leader Ahmad Shah Massoud issued a fatwa against bin Laden, calling for his death. Even though Sayyaf and Massoud were allied against the Taliban, Sayyaf and his group rejected the fatwa. Shortly after the fatwa was issued, Massoud and Sayyaf forces clashed violently, and one of Massoud's commanders was killed in the fighting. Yet fences were soon mended. Though the two leaders despised each other, they knew they needed one other if they were going to defeat the Taliban. A truce was quickly issued.

In October 2000, Able Danger reported that it suspected three people in the United States were planning a terrorist attack. All three were Al Qaeda members, and all three had trained in Sayyaf's camps. The DoD did nothing with this information.

Then in February of 2001, Sayyaf agreed to meet yet again with the Taliban leadership. He was offered a political position in the Taliban government, in exchange for "playing ball." Sayyaf refused the Taliban offer. While at this meeting—according to the US State Department (and many other organizations)—Sayyaf learned about the planned Al Qaeda attacks that would occur on September 11.

As September of 2001 drew ever closer, Sayyaf realized he was losing ground against the Taliban. It became clear to him that the only way he could hope to beat them would be with military and financial support from the United States. Sayyaf also realized that if the September 11 attacks went off as planned, US military would respond by raining hell on the Taliban. Yet after the smoke cleared, Sayyaf suspected Massoud would be placed in charge of the country. Sayyaf knew he could not let that happen.

On September 9, 2001, just two days before 9/11, Massoud was assassinated by two suicide bombers posing as journalists. While the west reported that Al Qaeda was likely behind Massoud's death, it was common knowledge in the Middle East—and was even reported by media outlets there—that the meeting between the suicide bombers and Massoud had been arranged by Sayyaf. This was true. In fact, Sayyaf had positioned himself right outside the tent when the bomb went off. He'd wanted to watch it happen.

Then, on September 11, 2001, bin Laden attacked the US, bringing down the Twin Towers in New York, severely damaging the Pentagon, and killing over three thousand people. Just as Sayyaf had predicted, one month later the United States invaded Afghanistan and gave tens of millions of dollars in financial and material support to Sayyaf to enable him to fight the Taliban.

During this time, members of Able Danger—who were upset that their report had been ignored and (in their opinion) could have prevented the attack—complained to the

Inspector General (IG). In this complaint, they included information about Sayyaf's connection to the attack. But something remarkable happened. Before the IG could see the evidence, the Defense Intelligence Agency (DIA) destroyed almost all of the records and data collected in the Able Danger operation. This rendered the alleged connection in the complaint toothless.

However, in April of 2005, Republican Representative Curt Weldon, vice chairman of the House Armed Services and House Homeland Security committees, got wind of the operation. He insisted that a formal investigation into Able Danger be conducted by the US Senate Intelligence Committee. And so it was. However, during the course of the investigation, the DIA prevented key personnel from testifying. That—coupled with the fact most of the documents salient to Able Danger operation had been destroyed—led the committee to conclude that the wilder assertions about Able Danger could not be confirmed. In its findings, the committee stated it had been unable to locate supporting evidence regarding "one of the most disturbing claims about the Sept. 11 terrorist strikes." That is, Sayyaf's connection.

The DIA assumed bin Laden was behind the attacks, and was correct in this assumption. However, by destroying the evidence that others might have also been involved or had foreknowledge, it made bin Laden the only guilty party. The only target. The US turned its attentions elsewhere. For the moment, it had bigger fish to fry. In just two short months after the invasion, the United States military and the Northern Alliance defeated the Taliban. Hamid Karzai would officially be made the President of Afghanistan by the US

While Abu Zubaydah now rots in a cell in Guantanamo, Sayyaf—who had foreknowledge of the 9/11 attacks, and could have informed the US, yet did nothing—remains a free man. More than that, he was assigned by the US to help write the new Afghan constitution, and was appointed to a high-ranking position in the Afghanistan parliament. He still occupies that position to this day.

Chapter Six

The Millennium Bomb Plot

The US government has made accusations and allegations about Abu Zubaydah that range from operating Jihadi training camps to outright involvement in terrorist operations targeting the United States. The government also has a long list of terrorists with whom they believe Abu Zubaydah was associated. Al Qaeda members figure prominently on this list. However, after reviewing the government documents relevant to Abu Zubaydah—many of which have become available through WikiLeaks—one cannot help but notice a trend in the wording. When the government discusses the people with whom Abu Zubaydah was associated, they consistently employ phrases such as "had supposed ties to," "is alleged to have known," or "is considered to be." Vitally, this same verbal prevarication is employed whenever Abu Zubaydah's ties to specific terrorist plots are discussed. They are consistently worded as: "is believed to have been involved in . . ." No hard evidence or proof is ever offered.

With one exception.

The US government claims firm and certain knowledge of Abu Zubaydah's involvement in a plot known as "The Millennium Attacks." These attacks were purportedly planned for December 31, 1999, and were supposed to take place in three locations simultaneously. Two of the locations were in Jordan—at the Radisson Hotel in Amman, and at a location in Mount Nebo (where it is believed Jesus was baptized by John the Baptist). Both locations are popular tourist attractions for Americans during the winter months. The third location picked to attack was Los Angeles International Airport (LAX).[57]

In October of 1998, the FBI received warnings of the possible attacks from Jordanian intelligence. The Jordanians believed several of the suspects involved in the plotting were American citizens, and for that reason a team of agents from the FBI's New York City field office was dispatched to follow up.

While the FBI was conducting its investigation, the CIA section chief at the Jordanian embassy also turned out to be looking into the matter. In November of 1998, the FBI sent findings to the Justice Department indicating that they believed the operation was being planned and funded by Al Qaeda, and that Abu Zubaydah was playing a major role. Around the same time, the CIA section chief in Jordan sent findings from his own investigation to the CIA headquarters in Langley, Virginia. Though the CIA report identified the some of the same suspects, its ultimate conclusions were very different. The CIA reported that the attacks were being funded and planned by Hamas and Hezbollah. The CIA said it thought Abu Zubaydah might have been in charge of providing travel to the training camps for the operatives involved, but that it was probable that he did not know the details of the operation. When Langley sent their reports to the Justice Department (twelve detailed reports in all), the Justice Department hastily decided the CIA investigation had erred, and discarded the twelve CIA reports provided by the section chief in Jordan.[58] According to retired FBI agent Ali Soufan, the reason the Justice Department discarded the CIA reports was because "if the intelligence didn't match, we (the US) would have difficulty prosecuting the case." So the big questions remains: Why was there such a big difference between the findings of the two agencies? Why did the Justice Department choose the FBI's report over the CIA's?

The FBI came to the conclusion that Al Qaeda was behind the attacks. This was not the case. In fact, all of the suspects were instead associated with the Islamic Union, an Egyptian branch of Hamas. It's an organization that the US and many other nations officially consider to be a terrorist organization. One significant aspect of this discrepancy is that Hamas—including its Egyptian branch—are mortal enemies of Al Qaeda. Several prominent Al Qaeda leaders like Osama bin Laden have been outspoken of their hatred of Hamas, repeatedly stating in public that they consider Hamas to be apostates to Muslim faith. Hamas reciprocates this hatred of Al Qaeda. It has executed members of Al Qaeda for the simple crime of accidentally trespassing into Hamas-held territory.

Though the CIA's intelligence involved most of the same suspects, its theory as to who might be behind the operation was very different. Its evidence and reasoning was different too.

Hezbollah and Hamas—though operating under different ideologies and beliefs—had worked together in the past, most notably in attacks in Jordan, Israel, and Lebanon.[59] Further, the suspects in this case all had links of one sort or another to the Islamic Union (and, therefore, Hamas). According to the FBI's findings, all of the suspects had been trained at the Khaldan Camp, Sayyaf's camp overseen by Abu Zubaydah. However, the CIA found that several of the suspects had instead been trained at a camp in the Bekaa Valley in Eastern Lebanon, which was a Hezbollah camp. Hezbollah and Al Qaeda are enemies, just as Hamas and Al Qaeda are.

Abu Zubaydah was practically unknown to US intelligence agencies until the plot for the Millennium Attack was discovered. His business relationships—those happening both above and below him—are significant in supporting the claim that it was Hamas and Hezbollah, not Al Qaeda, that were behind the attacks. One of Abu Zubaydah's associates who played a major role in the operation and is never mentioned in DoD documents is Kalil Al-Deek. According to hard-to-find FBI memoranda released prior to 9/11, a clear affiliation exists connecting Abu Zubaydah and Al-Deek, and this connection was well known by the US government.[60]

Al-Deek, was born in Jordan in 1957, and moved to the US in the 1980s to study computer science. Soon after arriving in Orange County, California, he married and became an American citizen. Al-Deek's friends considered him to be a kind and charitable man. Around 1991, Al-Deek began talking to a new neighbor who lived in his apartment building named Hisham Diab. Hisham Diab was from Egypt and had been living in the US since the late 1980s. Diab had radical views and interpretations of Islam, and held weekly meetings at his apartment with other known radicals such as Omar Abdel Rahman and Adam Yahiye Gadahn. Gadahn was an American-born citizen who had converted to Islam.[61] Omar Abdel Rahman was the leader of a group called the Islamic Union, which had many smaller splinter groups located across the United States and Canada. Rahman himself resided in New York City but spent most of his time traveling to group meetings, including those held at Diab's apartment and in Montreal, Canada.

Al-Deek found himself aligning fully with the radical ideology of the group. He began working as a staff member for a charity foundation called Islamic Association of Palestine (IAP). Shortly after 9/11, it was discovered that the organization regularly conducted fundraising activities which had directly supported Hamas and Hezbollah attacks against Israel. IAP was operated by an umbrella organization called the SAAR Foundation, which was run by Saudi Arabian billionaire Sheikh Sulaiman bin Abdul-Aziz Al-Rajhi. Al-Rajhi is currently the chairman of Al-Rajhi Bank, one of the largest companies in Saudi Arabia and the largest Islamic-owned bank in the world. As of 2011, his wealth was estimated by Forbes at $7.7 billion, making him the 120th wealthiest person in the world.

The Al-Rajhi family is Saudi Arabia's wealthiest non-royal family and among the world's leading philanthropists. However, in 1985, Al-Rajhi formed the SAAR Foundation, a charity front for Hamas activities. The SAAR's US headquarters opened in 1985 in Herndon, Virginia. The US office was headed up by Alamoudi, Khalil Al-Deek's personal friend.

Alamoudi had been born and raised in Yemen, moved to the US in 1979, and became an American citizen in 1996. Alamoudi was a busy man. Not only was he the CEO of the US office of the SAAR Foundation, in 1990 he founded a lobbyist group called the American Muslim Council. And in addition to his work with American Muslims, he had worked directly for the US government from 1990 to 2000, consulting on a project for the Pentagon involving the selection of

US Army Muslim Chaplains. In 1993, when Bill Clinton took office, Alamoudi also served as an Islamic Affairs Advisor on Clinton's staff and became a State Department Goodwill Ambassador to Muslim Nations. In early 2000, he and other Muslim leaders from the SAAR Foundation met with George W. Bush in Austin, Texas, offering financial support for his bid for the White House. In exchange, Alamoudi wanted Bush's commitment to repeal certain anti-terrorist laws. In addition to offering and contributing financial support to presidential candidate George W. Bush, Alamoudi became a personal friend of Karl Rove, the man who eventually became George W. Bush's presidential advisor. (It's still shocking that Alamoudi was ever able to get so cozy with so many political insiders so quickly.)

After the World Trade Center was attacked by Islamic fundamentalists to protest the US's support of Israel, Omar Abdel Rahman, who, despite not having been directly involved in the attack himself, was charged (on October 1, 1995) with helping to mastermind the attack and sentenced to life in prison in 1996. Numerous attempts to link Rahman to Al Qaeda have been made, though none have been successful. However, there is concrete evidence of Rahman's association with Abdul Rasul Sayyaf. Rahman and Sayyaf had attended college together in Egypt and were very close personal friends.

Sayyaf was outspoken about his old friend Rahman's conviction, publically calling it "a travesty of justice." In 1997, two followers of Rahman and Khalil Al-Deek began planning "millennium attacks" against the United States and Jordan. The two leaders of the planned attacks were Raed Hijazi, an American citizen born in California, and Abu Hoshar, a Palestinian. To prepare for the operation, they contacted Sayyaf's group. The Islamic Union agreed to support their training and they put Abu Zubaydah in charge of sending the individuals who would carry out the attacks to the Khaldan training camp. The attacks were funded by the organizations Al-Deek was working for—the Islamic Association of Palestine (IAP) and Charity Without Borders. In order to avoid suspicion by the US authorities, Al-Deek flew to Chicago to wire the funds to Abu Zubaydah, who was then living in Pakistan.

Al-Deek had successfully transferred funds in this manner for several months, but the FBI eventually became suspicious and began asking questions. To avoid generating continued FBI interest, Al-Deek moved to Pakistan and started an import/export company with Abu Zubaydah. Together they opened a joint business account with a Saudi Arabian bank in order to launder the funds from the IAP to Islamic Unity and fund the operation.[62] As ridiculous as it may sound today, on October 28, 2000, just two months prior to the planned Millennium Attacks, Alamoudi publicly admitted being a supporter of both Hamas and Hezbollah at a Muslim rally held in Washington DC (It is important to note that even after this admission, Alamoudi was made a guest at the White House on several occasions in 2001 and 2002, both before and after the 9/11 attacks. This was thanks in large part to his support for the Bush campaign.)

In November 1999, one month before the operation was supposed to occur, Jordanian intelligence intercepted a phone call from Abu Zubaydah to Khadr Abu Hoshar, the Palestinian extremist.

Abu Zubaydah told Hoshar, "The time for training is over."

Suspecting this was a signal to commence a terrorist attack in Jordan, Jordanian intelligence informed FBI agents already in Jordan about the phone call. Jordanian authorities then arrested Hoshar and twenty-five others on December

12. Pakistani authorities were then notified of the attacks, and the Pakistanis went after both Al-Deek and Abu Zubaydah.

Al-Deek was apprehended by Pakistani authorities on December 17, 1999, but Abu Zubaydah escaped. Al-Deek was extradited to Jordan for questioning about his role. The twenty-five other people arrested in Jordan were all tried and convicted for their participation in the plot. Twenty of them were sentenced to twenty years to life in prison. The others were sentenced to death. Abu Zubaydah, though not in custody, was sentenced to death *in absentia*. Even though all the suspects who were involved (or thought to be involved) in the plot received harsh sentences, Al-Deek was questioned by Jordanian intelligence and the FBI, then released without explanation or charges, returning to Pakistan in May of 2001.[63]

After 9/11, the Bush administration cracked down on Islamic foundations supporting terrorist groups. On March 20, 2002, the SAAR Foundation headquarters was raided by the FBI. The raid, known as Operation Green Quest, was conducted because the FBI had suspicions the organization was funding terrorist activities. Hundreds of financial documents were taken from the foundation's headquarters, but no arrests were made.

Muammar Gadhafi, former president of Libya, was a known supporter of and financier for Hamas activities. In 2003, he made arrangements with Alamoudi to travel to Libya to pick up $340,000 in US currency to fund a Hamas operation. Alamoudi went to Libya to pick up the cash. In September 2003, while making his way back to the US, British authorities arrested him at Heathrow Airport with the money.[64] In October of 2003, he was extradited to the US and three charges were formally brought against him—illegally accepting funds from Libya, tax evasion, and immigration fraud. In October 2004, Alamoudi was found guilty and convicted on all three charges. He is currently serving a twenty-three-year sentence in a federal penitentiary for his crimes.

Was Abu Zubaydah aware of and involved in these Millennium Attacks too? It is very probable. However, the exact degree of his involvement may never be known. It is further likely that the CIA would have downplayed his involvement—or ignored it entirely—because connecting these events to him would also connect the CIA back to prior operations by/with Abu Zubaydah that they hoped the world would soon forget.

Chapter Seven

Will The Real Abu Zubaydah Please Stand Up?

After the failed Millennium Attacks, Abu Zubaydah went on the run. The FBI and the CIA were both looking for him, and the RAND Corporation also began investigating Abu Zubaydah. From the information they had on hand, RAND created a biography of Abu Zubaydah which was then used by CIA and FBI operatives in the field. The problem was that most of RAND's information was completely wrong.

For example, RAND (and the CIA and FBI) believed of Abu Zubaydah that he:

- Had been born in Saudi Arabia, but grew up in the Gaza Strip of Palestine
- Had joined Hamas as a youngster
- Had been recruited in the 1980s by Egyptian Islamic Jihad leader Al-Zawahiri (a commander of Al Qaeda)
- Had fought directly against the Soviets
- Had become an Al Qaeda's operational chief in the 1990s

- Was married to a woman

After extensively interviewing Abu Zubaydah's family and studying his personal diaries, we now know that every point from the RAND file noted above is completely wrong. Abu Zubaydah didn't grow up in Palestine; he grew up in Saudi Arabia. He was never in Hamas, and did not meet Al-Zawahiri in his youth. He did not fight the Soviets in the late 1980s—he was still in high school in Saudi Arabia at that time. He was not in Al Qaeda, let alone their chief of operations. And he was never married.

Red flags should have been raised by these discrepancies when (after his eventual capture) the Pakistani media reported that the Taliban leadership was stating that the United States had captured "the wrong Abu Zubaydah." It is also evident that someone in the CIA still had questions about Abu Zubaydah's capture. Shortly after, Abu Zubaydah went into CIA custody and was rendered to a classified location for interrogation, the CIA's Counterterrorism Center, which was tasked with questioning Abu Zubaydah, did not immediately send anyone to interrogate him because they did not believe it was the correct Abu Zubaydah who had been captured. When interrogation did finally begin, his answers led many in the CIA to wonder whether they had the right person. However, none of this resulted in any substantive reevaluation by the CIA. Instead, Abu Zubaydah was simply counted "a tough egg to crack." The CIA concluded that he was lying to them intentionally. This, eventually, led to the decision to torture Abu Zubaydah.

So how did our top intelligence agencies formulate such distorted untruths?

It has never before been reported, but the fact is there *were indeed two Jihadi Abu Zubaydahs.*

The other one was named Maher Abu Zubayda, and they were cousins. Intelligence agencies, in a rush and unaware of this, had conflated their Abu Zubaydahs when piecing together dossiers. Discrepancies that should have been red flags were never raised because the CIA and FBI did not communicate effectively with one another, and because, before 9/11, both agencies did not have enough staff fluent in Arabic available to analyze critical information in the case.

There are other signs of a ball being dropped, too. Government documents concerning Abu Zubaydah spell his name several different ways. For example, some government documents spell his name Abu Zubaydah, while others list him as Zubaida, or Zbaida.

The name "Abu Zubaydah" is the family name of a large tribe with roots in Palestinian ancestry. Every member of that tribe could and likely did use the name "Abu Zubaydah" when culturally necessary and appropriate. Many individuals in Palestine and in the West Bank with origins in this family still use the name. The name itself is not common *per se,* but can be traced to the village of Yabna in Palestine that many claim as an ancestral home. The inhabitants of Yabna were uprooted by the Israeli military in 1948.[65] The "Abu Zubaydah" family was among the scattered. Today, the family populates the Gaza Strip in the refugee area of Bureij. It has been established that Zayn (the Abu Zubaydah in custody) and Maher share a common origin. Their use of the name "Abu Zubaydah" illustrates that their connection is likely through this Palestinian tribe. There does remain one striking difference between Zayn's (the Abu Zubaydah in custody), and Maher's use of the "Abu Zubaydah" name. While Abu Zubaydah typically spelled his name in English as "Abu Zubaydah" or "Abu Zubaida," Maher usually spelled his name in English as "Abu Zubaida" or "Abu Zbaida." Both spellings are derived from the same Arabic name, "أبوزيدة," which can be translated into English in many different ways. However, so long as the main vowels are present in the spellings, the name is always translated *back* to the aforementioned Arabic name. It is clear that both Zayn's and Maher's spellings share the main vowels. Thus, despite the difference of English spelling chosen by Zayn and Maher, both names reflect the *one* proper way to spell the name in Arabic. According to Seton Hall University School of Law's Center for Policy and Research Senior Fellow, Ghalib Mahmoud (who is from Palestine and is fluent in Arabic) the difference in spellings of the name does not indicate that they are from different families or tribes; in fact it reveals the opposite. As Ghalib stated in an interview:

> *"In considering the Palestinian tribe connection shared between Zayn and Maher as well as the fact that their spellings of the family name 'Abu Zubaydah' does not represent a separate origin, it becomes apparent that it could be possible to conflate, confuse, and combine the lives and identities of these two men."*

To avoid any confusion going forward, we will refer to the Abu Zubaydah in custody at Guantanamo as Abu Zubaydah, and Maher Abu Zubaydah simply as Maher.

So who was Maher?

Like Abu Zubaydah, Maher was born in Saudi Arabia. He is also the same age as Abu Zubaydah. However, Maher and his family moved to the Gaza Strip when he was still quite young. As a teen, Maher became active with Hamas, later met Al-Zawahiri, and joined the Egyptian Islamic Jihad (EIJ). He traveled to Pakistan the late 1980s and fought in Afghanistan against the Soviet army. All of which matches the biographical information of the Abu Zubaydah the US was looking for.

Maher drops off the radar then, but reappears in the United States in 1994, on a student visa. He had listed an address in San Jose, California, just three blocks from where a known Al Qaeda spy named Ali Mohammed was living.

Ali Abdul Saoud Mohamed, known as Ali Mohammed, had infiltrated the United States intelligence community while simultaneously working for Osama bin Laden. He worked under the direction of Ayman Mohammed Rabie al-Zawahiri[66] ("al-Zawahiri") as both an Egyptian EIJ agent, and a United States Army Sargent. Ali Mohamed—with the help of a colleague named Khaled Abu el-Dahab[67] ("el-Dahab")—created an Al Qaeda cell based in Santa Clara, California. Mohamed would later plead guilty to a role in the bombings of the US embassies in Kenya and Tanzania.[68]

The son of an Egyptian soldier,[69] Mohamed was born June 3, 1952.[70] Mohamed, who himself joined the Egyptian army in the early 1980s, was known for his both his great intelligence and physical strength.[71] While a member of the Egyptian army, Mohamed participated in a soldier exchange program with the United States Green Berets,[72] allowing him to travel to Fort Bragg and receive training in guerilla warfare.[73] Upon his return, Egypt experienced a regime change, and Mohamed, who let his frustration about how the Egyptian military was being run become public, was dismissed.[74]

After he was let go from the Egyptian Army, Mohamed became a security consultant for Egyptian Air.[75] He simultaneously joined the EIJ working directly with al-Zawahiri, thus beginning his career as one of the most infamous double agents of our era.[76] Mohamed went to the Egyptian government in Cairo and offered his services as infiltrator of the EIJ, despite actually being a member of EIJ.[77] Mohamed also went to the United States Central Intelligence Agency (CIA) and offered to go undercover and infiltrate mosques suspected of fomenting terrorist activities.[78] However, the CIA eventually learned of Mohamed's dual identity, dismissed him, and saw that he was placed on a US Department of Justice (DOJ) watch list.[79]

Despite being on the watch list, Mohamed was still able to legally obtain a United States visa and permanently relocate to the United States.[80] While on a flight bound for California, Mohamed met an American woman named Linda Sanchez. After a short courtship, the pair married and relocated to Santa Clara.[81]Mohamed enlisted in the United States army, where he was quickly promoted to sergeant and once again returned to Fort Bragg.[82] This time, Mohamed was assigned to a Special Forces unit.

Then, during a joint US and Egyptian training mission in 1987, Egyptian officials took US Army officials aside to warn them that they believed Mohamed was a Muslim extremist.[83] Based on this tip, the US Army elected to remove Mohamed from Special Forces upon his return to Fort Bragg. Even so, he was still permitted to remain in the Army.[84] In 1988, Mohamed informed his superior officer that he planned on using an upcoming leave to fight in the Afghanistan War against the Soviets.[85] Despite being explicitly directed not to do so, Mohamed traveled to Afghanistan and joined the fight anyway, eventually returning to Fort Bragg with a Soviet belt as a trophy.[86] His superiors were displeased, but no action was taken against him, and he was never censured.

In the early 1990s, Mohamed became connected to Osama bin Laden and Al Qaeda through his involvement with EIJ.[87] Mohamed would continue to work closely with bin

Laden, and conducted military and basic explosives training for Al Qaeda in Afghanistan whenever he was able. He also provided Al Qaeda with training documents stolen from the U.S. Army.[88] He became central to Al Qaeda's plan to infiltrate the United States.[89]

After living in San Jose for one year, Maher moved to Florida in 1995 to attend flight school, and soon received his pilot's license. It is still unclear precisely which flight school he attended, but it *is* known that Maher lived just one mile from Embry Riddle Aeronautical University Flight School in Daytona Beach, Florida, and just two and a half miles from one of the 9/11 highjackers, Waleed Al-Shehri. Maher also regularly visited a strip club in Daytona Beach called the Pink Pony, which was frequented by several of the 9/11 hijackers.

On August 11, 1995, while still in Florida, Maher got married after a very short courtship. Maher's wife (who has requested to remain anonymous and unnamed) was nice, good looking, and spoke English. But she was also young and naive. Maher's wife believed he was in the US on a student visa. He told her he was from Saudi Arabia, though she noticed that he had Jordanian travel documents. Soon after they were married, she began to suspect that her husband had misrepresented himself in more than one important way. She said that, in public, Maher would act like a drunk, boisterous American, but at home he would become strict, religious, and stern. He concealed from her the fact that he had a pilot's license, and that he sometimes worked as a pilot. Meanwhile, they were living in poverty. While Maher told his wife they could barely afford food, she saw bank statements in his name seeming to indicate that he had thousands of dollars squirrelled away. However, the statements were in Arabic—which she could not read—so she was never entirely sure. Maher seemed terrified that he would be deported to Jordan, and told his wife that he believed he would be killed by the Jordanian government if that happed. She stated that he would often leave her alone for days and weeks at a time, never indicating where he was going. She said he only had one friend. (Years later, when shown several photos of random US citizens by the US government, she positively identified Ali Mohamed as Maher's lone friend.) In the year 2000, Maher abandoned her completely, and did not inform her where he was going or why. Days after 9/11, the FBI pulled her out of work and questioned her for hours about Maher.

According to FOIA-accessible FBI documents, after Maher abandoned his wife, he moved to Montana. There, he bought a large ranch with six hundred and fifty thousand dollars in traveler's checks. The FBI believed that, for years, Al Qaeda had wanted to ignite massive forest fires in Montana and other Plains states. It was also suspected that Al Qaeda might attack dams or other infrastructure points in those areas.

The Fort Peck Dam was just twenty miles from Maher's ranch. One of the largest and most important dams in the United States, it has been estimated that if the Fort Peck Dam failed, thousands of acres of farmland would be rendered unusable by flooding.

Maher's Montana neighbors would later characterize him as a quiet man who often visited the diner and library in the nearest town. The librarian said that Maher would sit in the library for hours writing and studying books about Fort Peck Dam.

On September 10, 2001, an explosion occurred on Maher's ranch, and the house on the property burned down. Before the fire department could respond, Maher left the property. A week later, on September 19, 2001, Maher was arrested at a Best Western in Miles City, Montana, by border patrol agents. He had several firearms in his possession. Within hours of Maher's arrest, the FBI blocked all entrances to the Fort Peck Dam, and began to conduct an investigation. (The authors of this book have made several attempts—through FOIA requests and direct FBI contacts—to discover additional details about this investigation and what it revealed. All attempts and requests have been denied. In each case, national security issues were cited, with no further explanation given.)

After his arrest, Maher was moved to a federal holding facility in Billings where he was charged with unlawful possession of a firearm and multiple immigration violations. On March 28, 2002—just one day after his cousin, Abu Zubaydah, was captured in Afghanistan—Maher was convicted on these charges. He spent six months in a federal holding facility in Washington State, and was then deported. Court documents do not reveal what country he was deported to.

While Maher was in custody, the FBI was investigating the 9/11 attacks in an investigation codenamed PENTTBOMB (short for Pentagon World Twin Towers Bombing). The PENTTBOMB began just hours after the attacks on September 11, 2001, and became the largest FBI investigation ever conducted. Simply, the goal of PENTTBOMB was to learn the identities of everyone behind these terrorist attacks. FBI documents show that Maher was a suspect in the PENTTBOMB investigation. Even so, the information that a man named Abu Zubaydah (Maher) was arrested and in custody in the US never flowed their way. It was certainly never made available to the CIA and FBI agents risking their lives on the ground in Pakistan looking for Abu Zubaydah.

After Maher was deported, it was almost ten years before his new location began to reveal itself. In 2012, Abu Zubaydah's defense team received a letter from a man in Jordan named Mahmoud explaining in great detail that an "Abu Zubaydah" had been spotted in a prison just outside of Amman, Jordan, in 2005. This could not have been same the Abu Zubaydah that had been captured in Pakistan, because in 2005 he was then in a CIA rendition site in Poland. Before he could be questioned further by Abu Zubaydah's defense team, it was reported to them that Mahmoud was killed in a CIA drone strike.

It becomes increasingly clear, the harder one looks into this, that issues of identity become central to our attempts to understand Abu Zubaydah's fate, who he is, and how he arrived there. Whether the CIA had any sense of this—and *when* they had it—is another question entirely.

Chapter Eight

The Dead Pool

One cannot follow the trail of Abu Zubaydah's life without noticing that it is littered with bodies of dead men. Many of these dead are individuals who could have proved inconvenient for the CIA, which is keen to conceal the role it had played for so many years in nurturing the programs that had produced Mujahedeen fighters—fighters who had first fought the Soviets, but then turned their attention elsewhere. Many of these dead could have also provided information that might have exonerated Abu Zubaydah, or at least clarified the areas where he was or *was not* culpable. Instead, these men are dead.

The man who was the head trainer at the Khaldan training camp—the same man whom Abu Zubaydah refers to in his diaries as his best friend—Ibn al-Shaykh Al Libi, was captured in Afghanistan in November 2001, not long after the beginning of the US invasion. After being captured, he was interrogated by both the American and Egyptian forces. Al

Libi gave false information under torture to Egyptian interrogators. (The CIA now acknowledges this.) Nevertheless, that information was cited by the Bush administration in the months preceding the 2003 invasion of Iraq as evidence of an explicit connection between Saddam Hussein and Al Qaeda. In 2006, the United States transferred Al Libi from where he had been imprisoned in Afghanistan to new quarters in Libya. On May 19, 2009, the Libyan government reported that he had committed suicide by hanging himself in his cell. Human Rights Watch, which had previously sent two representatives to visit Al Libi, called for an investigation into the circumstances of his death. Several news outlets including the *New York Times* have alleged that Al Libi did not commit suicide, but was in fact murdered.

Three weeks after Al Libi's death, the US government reported that one of the men who had been with Abu Zubaydah during his capture, Ali Abdullah Ahmed, had died by hanging in his cell in Guantanamo on June 9, 2006. It was—hideously—the beginning of a trend. As of the time of this writing, all sixteen persons who were captured in the house with Abu Zubaydah and put into custody are confirmed dead.

Khalil Al-Deek—the associate of Abu Zubaydah who was captured and released by the Jordanian government for suspected involvement in one of the millennium bomb plots—was confirmed killed in April 2005. None of the details surrounding his death have ever been made public.

Carefully studying Abu Zubaydah's Guantanamo Bay Detainee Assessment Report (released by WikiLeaks) reveals that virtually all of Abu Zubaydah's known associates are also dead. The remarkable thing may not be that so many of them are no longer alive, but that Abu Zubaydah, somehow, is. The Guantanamo Bay Detainee Assessment Report is a classified document, but the function for which it exists is to account for why Abu Zubaydah is being held in US custody. According to that document, he is not accused of being a member of Al Qaeda. There is no evidence of such membership. And anyone who could have vouched for his membership has suffered an unnatural death.

Many of the corpses figuratively surrounding Abu Zubaydah are those of men of low birth and no particular status. But a few come from the highest echelons of power. Two of the dead are Saudi princes, and one was a Pakistani air marshal. After his capture, when CIA interrogators felt they were not getting actionable intelligence from Abu Zubaydah, they formulated a plan to get him to talk. They had him flown to a CIA black site in Afghanistan, but told him he was temporally being put into Saudi military custody for questioning by the Kingdom. In reality, he would be questioned by two Arab-American Green Berets disguised as Saudi soldiers. The interrogators believed Abu Zubaydah would be more likely to provide useful information in this scenario. Yet the plan backfired almost entirely.

Instead of being frightened, Abu Zubaydah was relieved and genuinely happy. He told the soldiers he knew three Saudi officials, and knew their cell phone numbers, and if the soldiers only would call them they'd order his release. The soldiers wrote down these numbers turned them over to the CIA. Shockingly, the phone numbers were in fact correct. One belonged to Ahmed bin Salman bin Abdul Aziz, a nephew of the Saudi King Fahd. A prominent man, he spent much of his time in the United States, and owned War Emblem—the horse that won the 2002 Kentucky Derby. Another number belonged to Chief Prince Turki Al-Faisal Bin Abdul Aziz. He was the man who had forged the agreement with Osama bin Laden in 1991 to fund Al Qaeda training inside

Sayyaf's camps. The third number belonged to the Pakistani air marshal Mushaf Ali Mir. He had close ties to Pakistani's Inter-Service Intelligence (ISI). US intelligence had long suspected that members of ISI had provided Al Qaeda with arms, supplies, and intelligence information.

After these names and numbers had been verified by the CIA, the agency shared that information with Saudi intelligence. Then all three men died.

On July 22, 2002, Prince Salman bin Abdul Aziz died of an apparent heart attack at age forty-three. A week later, Prince Turki Al-Faisal Bin Abdul Aziz was killed in a car crash. Then on February 20, 2003, Air Marshal Mushaf Ali Mir died in a plane crash while flying in clear weather.

How organic these accidents may have been is something not completely known.

And while the revelation of these subjects showed that Abu Zubaydah would disclose useful information under the correct circumstances, the US government seems not to have noticed. For reasons yet to be revealed, they chose to take another approach.

Chapter Nine

The Road to Torture

The FBI allows agents to take one of two approaches when conducting an interrogation. The Informed Interrogation Approach calls for the interrogator to become as fully informed on issues important to the subject as possible, and then to establish a rapport with the target. Under this approach, the interrogator builds trust over a period of time until the subject begins to supply useful information. In contrast, the Coercive Interrogation Approach—sometimes called the Coercive Interrogation Technique—calls for interrogators to employ force and pain, and to create a feeling of helplessness and isolation which will make the subject more likely to talk to his interrogator.

But the FBI would not be the only ones interrogating Abu Zubaydah.

Investigators for the Senate Select Committee on Intelligence found that the CIA, at the time of the 9/11 attacks, had in place "longstanding formal standards for conducting interrogations." These standards did not include torture or "enhanced techniques" of any kind. Indeed, according to the 2012 Senate Intelligence Committee report on CIA torture:

> *"In January 1989, the CIA informed the Committee that 'inhumane physical or psychological techniques are counter-productive because they do not produce intelligence and will probably result in false answers.' Testimony of the CIA deputy director for operations in 1988 (Richard Stolz) denounced coercive interrogation techniques, stating, '[p]hysical abuse or other degrading treatment was rejected, not only because it is wrong, but because it has historically proven to be ineffective.' By October 2001, CIA policy was to comply with the Depart-ment of the Army Field Manual 'Intelligence Interrogation.' A CIA Directorate of Operations Handbook from October 2001 states that the CIA does not engage in 'human rights violations,' which it defined as: 'Torture, cruel, inhuman, degrading treatment or punishment, or prolonged detention without charges or trial.' The handbook further stated that '[i]t is CIA policy to neither participate directly in nor encourage interrogation which involves the use of force, mental or physical torture, extremely demeaning indignities or exposure to inhu-mane treatment of any kind as an aid to interrogation.'"[90]*

Yet the rules that had worked so well in the past didn't seem to fit the world of late 2001, at least according to the CIA leadership. By November 2001, CIA Director George Tenet had ordered his attorneys and senior officers of the Agency's Counterterrorism Center to draft new protocols for inter-rogation that would allow for harsher approaches than the Agency had ever allowed before.

In a classified memo entitled "Hostile Interrogations: Le-gal Considerations for CIA Officers," dated November 21,

2001, "the Israeli example" is cited as a possible basis for arguing before courts and the American people that "torture was necessary to prevent imminent, significant, physical harm to persons, where there is no other available means to prevent the harm."[91]

But the CIA was already on record with the Senate Intelligence Committee as saying that torture didn't work. Committee investigators wrote, "Despite the CIA's previous statements that coercive physical and psychological interrogation techniques 'result in false answers' and have 'proven to be ineffective.'"[92] Nonetheless, by the end of November 2001, CIA attorneys began circulating a draft memorandum suggesting "novel" legal defenses for CIA officers who might, in the future, engage in torture. According to Senate investigators, "The memorandum stated that the 'CIA could argue that the torture was necessary to prevent imminent, significant, physical harm to persons, where there is no other available means to prevent the harm,' adding that 'states may be very unwilling to call the US to task for torture when it resulted in saving thousands of lives.'"[93]

Still, it wasn't up to the CIA's leadership to decide when and if torture should be employed. That remained a policy decision, and it would have to have the support of the Principals' Committee, chaired by the President, and including the Vice President, the National Security Advisor, the Attorney General, and the Secretaries of State and Defense—in addition to the CIA Director.

In January 2002, according to Senate investigators, the principals began debating whether to apply Geneva Convention protections to captured prisoners from Al Qaeda and the Taliban. Director Tenet sent a letter to President Bush urging "that the CIA be exempt from any application of these protections," arguing that application of Geneva would significantly hamper the ability of the CIA to obtain critical threat information necessary to save American lives.[94] On February 1, 2002—approximately two months prior to the detention of the CIA's first prisoner—a CIA attorney wrote that if CIA detainees were covered by Geneva there would be "few alternatives to simply asking questions." The attorney concluded that, if that were the case, "then the optic becomes how legally defensible is a particular act that probably violates the convention, but ultimately saves lives."[95]

Preparations for implementing a torture program thus pre-dated Abu Zubaydah's capture by many months. Senior CIA officers had already bought into the use of "Ticking Time Bomb" scenarios, in which it was argued that captured terrorists had to be tortured to reveal the locations of operations still underway that might result in the deaths of innocent people. However, as FBI agent and interrogator Ali Soufan would later testify before the Senate Judiciary Committee, these scenarios never actually arise. But that didn't stop the CIA's senior-most officials from creating a list of torture techniques, euphemistically called "enhanced interrogation techniques," to be used on high-profile prisoners.

According to the CIA's inspector general at the time, "the capture of senior Al Qaeda operative Abu Zubaydah on 27 March 2002 presented the Agency with the opportunity to obtain actionable intelligence on future threats to the United States from the most senior Al Qaeda member in US custody at the time. This accelerated CIA's development of an interrogation program."[96]

That development took the form of two CIA contract psychologists, Bruce Jessen and James Mitchell. Jessen and Mitchell had been psychologists with the US Air Force Survival, Evasion, Resistance, and Escape (SERE) school, where military personnel are exposed to the kinds of intense and hostile interrogation techniques to which they might be subjected if they were to be shot down and fall into enemy hands. The two founded a consulting company in 2005 to offer the CIA, apparently through a friend who worked in the CIA's Office of Technical Services, a "reverse-engineered" version of SERE training that could be carried out on prisoners to force them to talk. Senate investigators noted that neither Jessen nor Mitchell had any firsthand experience as interrogators, "nor did either have specialized knowledge of Al Qaeda, a background in terrorism, or any relevant regional, cultural, or linguistic expertise. Jessen had reviewed research on 'learned helplessness,' in which individuals might become passive and depressed in response to adverse or uncontrollable events. He theorized that inducing such a state could encourage a detainee to cooperate and provide information."[97] Yet it was Jessen and Mitchell who first suggested a list of ten coercive techniques that would be used on prisoners.

CIA officers then sent this list of techniques to the Justice Department's Office of Legal Counsel (OLC) for clearance. OLC attorney John Yoo drafted a series of memos approving each of the proposed techniques as legal. OLC director and assistant attorney general Jay Bybee signed the memos in early August 2002 after clearing them with attorneys on the National Security Council. Vice President Richard Cheney later confirmed that he "and others" had "signed off" on the torture techniques.[98] For the first time in US history, it was now legal to torture prisoners.

The CIA's torture techniques—ten in total—increased in severity as one went down the list. They were largely modeled on techniques used by Chinese communists against captured American servicemen during the Korean War, according to Senator Carl Levin, former chairman of the Senate Armed Services Committee.[99] As outlined in the CIA Inspector General's Report, they included Attention Grasp; Walling; Facial Hold; Facial Slap or Insult Slap; Cramped Confinement; Insect Placement; Wall Standing; Stress Positioning; Sleep Deprivation; and Waterboarding:

1. The attention grasp consists of grasping the detainee with both hands, with one hand on each side of the collar opening, in a controlled and quick motion. In the same motion as the grasp, the detainee is drawn toward the interrogator.

2. During the walling technique, the detainee is pulled forward and then quickly and firmly pushed into a flexible false wall so that his shoulder blades hit the wall. His head and neck are supported with a rolled towel to prevent whiplash.

3. The facial hold is used to hold the detainee's head immobile. The interrogator places an open palm on either side of the detainee's face and the interrogator's fingertips are kept well away from the detainee's eyes.

4. With the facial or insult slap, the fingers are slightly spread apart. The interrogator's hand makes contact with the area between the tip of the detainee's chin and the bottom of the corresponding earlobe.

5. In cramped confinement, the detainee is placed in a confined space, typically a small or large box, which is usually dark. Confinement in the smaller space lasts no more than two hours and in the larger space it can last up to eighteen hours.

6. Insects placed in a confinement box involve placing a harmless insect in the box with the detainee. [Authors' Note: This was to enhance the mental strain on prisoners like Abu Zubaydah, who had an irrational fear of insects.]

7. During wall standing, the detainee may stand about four to five feet from a wall with his feet spread approximately to his shoulder width. His arms are stretched out in front of him and his fingers rest on the wall to support all of his body weight. The detainee is not allowed to reposition his hands or feet.

8. The application of stress positions may include having the detainee sit on the floor with his legs extended straight out in front of him with his arms raised above his head or kneeling on the floor while leaning back at a 45 degree angle.

9. Sleep deprivation will not exceed eleven days at a time.

10. The application of the waterboard technique involves binding the detainee to a bench with his feet elevated above his head. The detainee's head is immobilized and an interrogator places a cloth over the detainee's mouth and nose while pouring water onto the cloth in a controlled manner. Airflow is restricted for twenty to forty seconds and the technique produces the sensation of drowning and suffocation.

The problem with these techniques is that—the opinions of John Yoo and Jay Bybee notwithstanding—they were specifically prohibited by law. The Federal Torture Act, 18 US Code § 2340, clearly defines torture:[100]

1. "torture means an act committed by a person acting under the color of law specifically intended to inflict severe physical or mental pain or suffering (other than pain or suffering incidental to lawful sanctions) upon another person within his custody or physical control;

2. "Severe mental pain or suffering" means the prolonged mental harm caused by or resulting from—

a. the intentional infliction of threatened infliction of severe physical pain or suffering;

b. the administration or application, or threatened administration or application, of mind-altering substances or other procedures calculated to disrupt profoundly the senses or the personality;

c. the threat of imminent death; or

d. the threat that another person will imminently be subjected to death, severe physical pain or suffering, or the administration or application of mind-altering substances or other procedures calculated to disrupt profoundly the senses or personality; and

3. "United States" means the several States of the United States, the District of Columbia, and the commonwealths, territories, and possessions of the United States.

The remainder of the Act could not be any clearer:

a. Offense.—
Whoever outside the United States commits or attempts to commit torture shall be fined under this title or imprisoned not more than 20 years, or both, and if death results to any person from conduct prohibited by this subsection, shall be punished by death or imprisoned for any term of years or for life.

b. Jurisdiction.—There is jurisdiction over the activity prohibited in subsection (a) if—
1. the alleged offender is a national of the United States; or
2. the alleged offender is present in the United States, irrespective of the nationality of the victim or alleged offender.

c. Conspiracy.—
A person who conspires to commit an offense under

this section shall be subject to the same penalties (other than the penalty of death) as the penalties prescribed for the offense, the commission of which was the object of the conspiracy.

The ten approved methods seem to meet the criteria for torture even when applied exactly as described. Yet the CIA officers involved did not always adhere strictly to the techniques. At least two prisoners were killed by CIA officers (or persons acting on behalf of the CIA) during interrogations. These instances—and many more near misses—often involved variations on the ten approved methods.

It wasn't just US law that prohibited what the CIA was doing. The United Nations Convention against Torture and Other Cruel, Inhuman, or Degrading Treatment or Punishment—of which the United States was the primary author and an original signatory—specifically bans anything approaching "enhanced interrogation" techniques. As Article 1 of the convention states:

> *"torture means any act by which severe pain or suffering, whether physical or mental, is intentionally inflicted on a person for such purposes as obtaining from him or a third person information or a confession, punishing him for an act he or a third person has committed or is suspected of having committed, or intimidating or coercing him or a third person, or for any reason based on discrimination of any kind, when such pain or suffering is inflicted by or at the instigation of or with the consent of acquiescence of a public official or other person acting in an official capacity.*"[101]

There was precedent for punishing Americans involved in torture, and specifically for involvement in waterboarding.

On January 21, 1968, the *Washington Post* ran a front-page photograph of an American soldier waterboarding a North Vietnamese prisoner. On the day that the photo was published, Defense Secretary Robert McNamara ordered an investigation, and the soldier eventually was court martialed and convicted of torturing a prisoner. [102]

The government had found waterboarding to be an inappropriate form of torture as recently as 1968. No law had been changed since. The Bush Administration merely pretended—thirty-four years later—that this and other precedents did not exist.

President George W. Bush approved the torture of Abu Zubaydah in writing on August 1, 2002. However, it turned out that there was already a backstory, and the torture had already begun, apparently *in anticipation* of the President's approval.

The CIA had flown Abu Zubaydah from Pakistan to his "onward location," a secret prison in a foreign country, code-named Detention Site Green, in late March 2002. He was too severely wounded to be questioned initially, however, and the Johns Hopkins physician had set up shop on the scene to care for his charge. The CIA medical team decided after his arrival that they could not handle the severity of his injuries, and Abu Zubaydah was again moved to a hospital for treatment. FBI Agent Ali Soufan recalled before the Senate Judiciary Committee: "At the hospital, we continued our questioning as much as possible, while taking into account his medical condition and the need to know all information he might have on existing threats."[103]

Some weeks later, Abu Zubaydah had recovered enough to be interrogated. As Soufan told the Senate Judiciary Committee:

"Immediately after Abu Zubaydah was captured, a fellow FBI agent and I were flown to meet him at an undisclosed location. We were both very familiar with Abu Zubaydah and have successfully interrogated Al Qaeda terrorists. We started interrogating him, supported by CIA officials who were stationed at the location, and within the first hour of the interrogation, using the Informed Interrogation Approach, we gained important actionable intelligence. The information was so important that, as I learned later from open sources, it went to CIA Director George Tenet, who was so impressed that he initially ordered us to be congratulated."[104]

Traditional FBI techniques were working. Those techniques instructed agents to "know your subject, establish a rapport with him, and engage him in conversation." This was happening, and it was yielding results. Soufan told the Senate Judiciary Committee that when Abu Zubaydah returned to the secret site from the hospital: "We were once again very successful and elicited information regarding the role of Khalid Shaikh Muhammad as the mastermind of the 9/11 attacks, and lots of other information that remains classified. It is important to remember that before this, we had no idea of KSM's role in 9/11 or his importance in the Al Qaeda leadership structure. All this happened before the CTC team (the CIA's Counterterrorism Center) arrived."

This was pivotal information. The CIA had had no idea that Khalid Shaikh Muhammad had been the mastermind of the September 11 attacks. They knew only that an individual named "Mukhtar" had been in charge at the time. Muhammad was on the FBI's most wanted list because he had been indicted in 1996 for his role in a plot to detonate explosives on twelve US airliners flying over the Pacific. On April 10, 2002, during an interrogation conducted by Soufan, Abu Zubaydah identified a photograph of Muhammad as "Mukhtar" and said, correctly, that he was a relative of Ramzi Ahmed Yousef, who was in a US prison after having detonated a bomb at the World Trade Center in 1993.

According to Senate investigators in the Senate torture report released in December 2014, "Abu Zubaydah told the FBI officers that Mukhtar trained the 9/11 hijackers and also provided additional information on KSM's background, to include that KSM spoke fluent English, was approximately 34 years old, and was responsible for Al Qaeda operations outside Afghanistan."[105] It was the FBI and Soufan that collected this critical information. There was no CIA involvement. But interestingly, Senate investigators noted, "Subsequent representations on the success of the CIA's Detention and Interrogation Program consistently describe Abu Zubaydah's identification of KSM's role in the September 11, 2001 attacks, as well as his identification of KSM's alias (Mukhtar), as being 'important' and 'vital' information."[106] The CIA was taking credit for the FBI's success.

Actionable intelligence notwithstanding, the CTC team's arrival presaged a sea change in the treatment of Abu Zubaydah.

Unbeknownst to Soufan and his FBI colleagues, a decision had been made in Washington that would change everything. The President had signed the order allowing Abu Zubaydah's torture to begin, and the CTC team already on its way to the site included untrained interrogators and also Jessen and Mitchell, who had created the torture program by reverse-engineering the SERE training.

As Soufan told the Senate Judiciary Committee:

"A few days after we started interrogating Abu Zubaydah, the CTC interrogation team finally arrived from DC with a contractor who was instructing them on how they should conduct the interrogations, and we (the FBI) were removed. Immediately, on the instructions of the contractor, harsh techniques were introduced, starting with nudity.

"The new techniques did not produce results as Abu Zubaydah shut down and stopped talking. At that time, nudity and low-level sleep deprivation (between 24 and 48 hours) was being used. After a few days of getting no information, and after repeated inquiries from DC asking why all of a sudden no information was being transmitted, when before there had been a steady stream, we were again given control of the interrogation."[107]

Soufan soon returned to his Informed Interrogation Approach. Abu Zubaydah, again clothed and with a good night's sleep, started talking. He gave the FBI details on Jose Padilla, the so-called "dirty bomber" whom Abu Zubaydah said was planning to detonate a radiological bomb. Thanks to this information, Padilla was arrested in Chicago, charged with criminal conspiracy, convicted, and eventually sentenced to twenty-one years in a federal prison.

But that wasn't good enough for the CIA, and the contractor again began using torture techniques, this time employing constant loud noise and temperature manipulation, in addition to nudity and sleep deprivation. Soufan and a fellow FBI agent objected to this, but were overruled. A CIA psychologist who had objected earlier left the site in protest.[108] The harsher techniques failed—again—and Soufan was once more asked to reengage with Abu Zubaydah. He had been traumatized by the torture techniques, but, eventually, Abu Zubaydah began speaking with Soufan.

While this was happening, Soufan sent formal objections to both FBI Headquarters and CIA Headquarters. In a cable to his leadership, he said that the CIA psychologist:

"believe[s] AZ is offering 'throw away information' and holding back from providing threat information. (It should be note [sic] that we have obtained critical information regarding AZ thus far and have now got him speaking about threat information, albeit from his hospital bed and not [an] appropriate interview environment for full follow-up (due to his health). Suddenly the psychiatric team here wants AZ to only interact with their [CIA officer] as being the best way to get the threat information...We offered several compromise solutions...all suggestions were immediately declined without further discussion...This again is quite odd as all information obtained from AZ has come from FBI lead interviewers and questioning...I have spent an un-calculable [sic] amount of hours at [Abu Zubaydah's] bedside assisting with medical help, holding his hand and comforting him through various medical procedures, even assisting him in going [to] the bathroom... We have built tremendous [rapport] with AZ and now that we are on the eve of 'regular' interviews to get threat information, we have been 'written out of future interviews'."[109]

The CIA tactics had shifted once more. Rather than sitting across a table from Soufan, Abu Zubaydah was now interrogated by CIA officers wearing all black uniforms—which included boots, gloves, balaclavas, and goggles—to keep Abu Zubaydah from identifying the officers, as well as to prevent him from "seeing the guards as individuals who he may attempt to establish a relationship or dialogue with."[110] Meanwhile, Abu Zubaydah was kept naked, deprived of sleep, and after being returned to Detention Site Green from the hospital, kept in a small white room with no windows and four halogen lights.

The CIA-FBI pissing match was coming to a head. The contractor again insisted on taking over, and he asked CIA Headquarters for permission to put Abu Zubaydah into what was called a "confinement box." Accordingly, Soufan again protested to his superiors at the FBI. He refused to further assist in interrogating Abu Zubaydah. FBI Director Robert Mueller agreed with Soufan's assessment—that the CIA's techniques constituted torture—and ordered that all FBI personnel return to the US.[111]

By the summer of 2002, the CIA was fully in control of Abu Zubaydah's fate. In June 2002, the CIA team decided to put Abu Zubaydah into isolation (solitary confinement) where he remained for forty-seven days. This isolation ended on August 4, 2002, after the President signed the memorandum allowing torture.

The problem for the CIA was that Abu Zubaydah was not providing actionable intelligence on Al Qaeda's next attack. This was because he simply didn't know any further information. But the "good cops" were out, while Jessen, Mitchell, and the "bad cops" were in. The CIA saw Abu Zubaydah's inability to provide the information as "unwillingness," and deemed him "uncooperative."

It was this determination that Abu Zubaydah was only being uncooperative that convinced CIA Headquarters to employ increasingly severe forms of interrogation upon their subject. As US Senate investigators subsequently found, in July of 2002 the CIA's leadership held several meetings specifically to discuss the use of "novel interrogation methods" on Abu Zubaydah.[112] These were the "enhanced interrogation techniques" that had previously been cleared by the Justice Department.

It was during this period, at the end of July 2002, that a senior officer at the Counterterrorism Center approached John Kiriakou and asked if he wanted to be "certified in the use of enhanced interrogation techniques."

"What's that mean?" Kiriakou asked in the moment.

"It means we're going to start getting rough with these guys!" was the immediate response.

The CTC officer quickly explained the new techniques that were in the offing.

"That sounds an awful lot like torture," Kiriakou said.

But then he added that he would take a couple of hours to think about it.

Kiriakou made an appointment to see a very senior CIA officer with whom he'd had a friendly relationship for a decade. That same afternoon he went to the seventh floor, the CIA's executive level, for the meeting. A moment after sitting down, he told the senior officer about the approach from CTC.

"What do you think?" he asked.

The response was not what he'd been expecting.

"First let's call it what it is," the senior officer said. "It's torture. They can use any euphemism they want, but it's still torture. And torture is a slippery slope. Eventually, somebody is going to go overboard and they're going to kill a prisoner. When that happens, there's going to be a Congressional investigation. Then there's going to be a Justice Department investigation. And in the end, somebody's going to go to prison. Do you want to go to prison?"

Kiriakou didn't.

Kiriakou walked back down to CTC, found the officer, and said bluntly: "This is a torture program. I don't want to be associated with it."

But others did.

More than a dozen CIA officers accepted the invitation to be trained in the new techniques. This dozen became the core cadre of "interrogators," a designation the CIA had never had before.

Yet prior to the actual torture beginning, the CIA found it had more paperwork to take care of. Following the July meetings, the CTC General Counsel and other CIA legal officials sent a letter to Attorney General John Ashcroft asking for a formal declination letter. This would be a letter from the Justice Department specifically declining to prosecute any CIA officer, or any person working on behalf of the CIA, "who may employ methods in the interrogation of Abu Zubaydah that otherwise might subject those individuals to prosecution."[113] The letter would also specify that "the interrogation team had concluded that the use of more aggressive methods is required to persuade Abu Zubaydah to provide the critical information we need to safeguard the lives of innumerable innocent men, women, and children within the United States and abroad." It concluded, tellingly, that these "aggressive methods" would otherwise be prohibited by the torture statute.[114]

The CIA knew that what they were planning to do was torture. They admitted as much in this letter. That was why they were asking for a "Get out of Jail Free" card for their torturers.

In a follow-up meeting between CIA attorneys and the Justice Department—and also in a letter from Deputy Assistant Attorney General John Yoo to CIA Acting General Counsel John Rizzo—Yoo advised that "the criminal prohibition on torture would not prohibit the methods proposed by the interrogation team because of the absence of any specific intent to inflict severe physical or mental pain or suffering." Such provisions, Yoo said, were central to the definition of torture.[115] This was unprecedented. There was no case law to support the Yoo/Bybee memos. The prohibition on torture was clear. It had always been clear. Yet the CIA, with the administration's full support, went forward anyway.

But there *were* objections. National Security Advisor Condoleezza Rice and Deputy National Security Advisor Stephen Hadley asked the Justice Department to delay final approval of the techniques "until the CIA provided specific details on its proposed interrogation techniques and an explanation of why the CIA is confident these techniques will not cause lasting and irreparable harm to Abu Zubaydah." Rice wanted a detailed explanation of what each technique entailed, and to see empirical data on the likelihood of lasting mental harm arising from waterboarding.[116]

Rice said later that she and John Bellinger III, her top legal advisor at both the National Security Council and later at the State Department, asked Attorney General Ashcroft to "personally review the legal guidance" that Yoo had provided to the CIA indicating that the program was legal.[117] In response, CIA and Justice Department officials spoke with representatives of the Department of Defense's Joint Personnel Recovery Agency (JPRA), which is responsible for providing SERE training, to ask about the long-term effects of SERE techniques in training exercises. In the end, Rice and Bellinger were satisfied with the response from the CIA and the Justice Department. Neither organization further objected to the techniques' use.

Meanwhile, the CIA, fully cognizant of what it was getting into, set about making contingency plans for Abu Zubaydah's potential death in custody. Senate investigators reported on a July 15, 2002 cable to CIA Headquarters from Detention Site Green that read:

"If [Abu Zubaydah] develops a serious medical condition which may involve a host of conditions including a heart attack or other catastrophic type of condition, all efforts will be made to ensure that proper medical care will be provided to [him]. In the event [Abu Zubaydah] dies, we need to be prepared to act accordingly, keeping in mind the liaison equities involving our hosts."

If he were to die in custody, the cable said, Abu Zubaydah would be cremated and scattered.

It went on.

"...regardless which [disposition] option we follow, however, and especially in light of the planned psychological techniques to be implemented, we need to get reasonable assurances that [Abu Zubaydah] will remain in isolation and incommunicado for the remainder of his life."[118]

CIA Headquarters responded similarly.

*"There is a fairly unanimous sentiment within HQS that [Abu Zubaydah] will never be placed in a situation where he has any significant contact with others and/or has the opportunity to be released. While it is difficult to discuss specifics at this point, all major players are in concurrence that **[Abu Zubaydah] should remain incommunicado for the remainder of his life.** [Our emphasis] This may preclude [Abu Zubaydah] from being turned over to another country, but a final decision regarding his future incarceration condition has yet to be made."*[119]

The importance of this CIA response cannot be overstated. Here we see the agency laying out explicitly that it is aware it is going to torture Abu Zubaydah, and that this means he may never be released from custody. If he is tortured, then he will never be released.

At the time of this writing, Abu Zubaydah remains in custody.

On July 24, 2002, John Ashcroft verbally approved the use of all the CIA torture techniques, with the exception of the waterboard, according to Senate investigators.[120] The interrogation team elected to wait until the waterboard was approved by Ashcroft, two days later, before using any of the techniques on Abu Zubaydah.

Legal cover was still on the minds of the CIA's leaders. On August 3, 2002, Headquarters sent a cable to the interrogation team at Detention Site Green, saying that the Justice Department's decision to allow the use of torture was "predicated upon the determinations by the interrogation team that Abu Zubaydah continues to withhold critical threat information."[121] In other words, the entire torture program was based on whether or not the torturers reported back to Headquarters that it was working.

The problem, however, was that there was a very basic disconnect between the goals of CIA Headquarters and the goals of the CIA interrogators. Headquarters wanted the details of Al Qaeda's next attack against the United States. However, the interrogators believed that the objective of the torture techniques was not, in fact, to persuade Abu Zubaydah to give up threat information. Instead, it was to confirm that Abu Zubaydah did not have any further threat information to give.[122]

Senate investigators would later note that "the interrogation team later deemed the use of the CIA's enhanced interrogation techniques a success, not because it resulted in critical threat information, but because it provided further evidence that Abu Zubaydah had not been withholding the aforementioned information from the interrogators."[123] This paradox should be terrifying to any sane person. If Abu Zubaydah had had threat information, Headquarters would have demanded that the torture continue in order that he be forced to give it up. And if he hadn't had threat information, Detention Site Green interrogators would have demanded that the torture continue to prove that he *didn't* have it to give up. No matter what, torture would be the right thing to do.

CIA leaders began preparing talking points concerning the torture program, including waterboarding, to be used to brief President Bush. According to Senate investigators, White House Counsel Alberto Gonzales later eliminated any mention of waterboarding, and in the end, the briefing never took place. Instead, an NSC attorney told Tenet's chief of staff that "the DCI had policy approval to employ the CIA's enhanced interrogation techniques."[124] The CIA's leadership chose to just assume that the President understood the program, and not to risk briefing him on it.

CIA Acting General Counsel John Rizzo believed that a year later—in July of 2003—the President still had not been briefed on the program, but that he would be eventually, "as part of the regular annual (covert action) review."[125] However, that never happened. In May of 2004, CIA Inspector General John Helgerson made a recommendation to Tenet that he should, finally, "brief the President regarding the implementation of the Agency's detention and interrogation activities pursuant to the MON (Memorandum of Notification) of 17 September 2001 or any other authorities (permissions), including the use of EITs and the fact that detainees have died. This Recommendation is significant." Tenet's response was, more or less, to tell the Inspector General to go jump in a lake. He informed the Inspector General that "the DCI will determine whether and to what extent the President requires a briefing on the Program."[126] But informed president or uninformed president, the CIA already had what it needed by mid-2002—policy approval.

On August 3, 2002, CIA Headquarters told Detention Site Green that its officers had permission to begin torturing Abu Zubaydah. The rules were clear, at least in the beginning. Only Jessen and Mitchell were to have direct contact with him. Everybody else, including medical personnel and other interrogators with whom he had had contact, were to be kept on the sidelines.[127]

Abu Zubaydah's torture began in earnest on August 4, 2002. From that date through August 23, according to Senate investigators, he was subjected to the entire spectrum of torture techniques that had been approved. Initially, Abu Zubaydah was stripped naked, shackled, and hooded.[128] Then, without saying a word, his interrogators placed a rolled towel around his neck and slammed him against a concrete wall. This action, on the very first day of the torture, was a violation of the Justice Department guidelines and was illegal. The interrogator later acknowledged that the collar was used to slam Abu Zubaydah against a concrete wall, not a cushioned plywood wall (as was called for), but no action was ever taken against him.[129]

Senate investigators found:

"The interrogators then removed the hood, performed an attention grab, and had Abu Zubaydah watch while a large confinement box was brought into the cell and laid on the floor. A cable states Abu Zubaydah was 'unhooded and the large confinement box was carried into the interrogation room and p[l]aced on the floor so as to appear like a coffin.' The interrogators then demanded detailed and verifiable

information on terrorist operations planned against the
United States, including the names, phone numbers, email
addresses, (and locations of) weapons caches, and safe houses
of anyone involved. CIA records describe Abu Zubaydah as
appearing apprehensive. Each time Abu Zubaydah denied
having additional information, the interrogators would per-
form a facial slap or face grab."[130]

But Abu Zubaydah didn't have any actionable threat information, and he couldn't provide what the interrogators wanted.
The information that Headquarters analysts were interested
in—such as the identification of "Mukhtar," the names of the
Arabs trained in Khaldan, and the structure of terrorist cells
around the world—were things he had already given to FBI
agent Soufan, with whom he had an established rapport.

But the interrogators had no intention of backing off.
At 6:20 p.m. on August 4, 2002 (the Senate investigators
reported), Abu Zubaydah was waterboarded for the first
time. "Over a two-and-a-half hour period, Abu Zubaydah
coughed, vomited, and had 'involuntary spasms of the torso
and extremities' during waterboarding."[131]

The questions from interrogators were variations on a
single theme: Where is the next attack going to happen? As
one of the interrogators later told the CIA Inspector General, his "instructions from [the Detention Site Green Chief of
Base] were to focus only on one issue, that is, Abu Zubaydah's knowledge of plans to attack the US."[132]

Meanwhile, the waterboarding continued.

In an email to the leadership of the CIA's Office of Medical Services ghoulishly titled, "And So It Begins," a medical
officer working on-site related that "The sessions accelerated
rapidly and progressed quickly to the water board after large
box, walling, and small box periods. [Abu Zubaydah] seems

very resistant to the water board. Longest time with the cloth over his face so far has been 17 seconds. This is sure to increase shortly. NO useful information so far...He did vomit a couple of times during the water board with some rice and beans. It's been 10 hours since he ate so this is surprising and disturbing. We plan to feed only Ensure for a while now. I'm head[ing] back for another water board session."[133]

By August 9, 2002, the interrogation team reported to CIA Headquarters that they had come to a "collective preliminary assessment" that it was "highly unlikely" that Abu Zubaydah "had actionable new information about current threats to the United States."[134] Yet this did nothing to stop what was happening. The constant torture, using all techniques available to the CIA, continued, twenty-four-hours a day, until August 20. By that date, Abu Zubaydah had become a psychologically broken person. Daily cables from Detention Site Green to CIA Headquarters reported that Abu Zubaydah frequently "cried, begged, pleaded, and whimpered," but continued to deny that he knew anything about an imminent threat to the United States.[135] The interrogators were no closer to foiling a terrorist plot—or even to determining whether there *was* a terrorist plot to foil—than they had been when Abu Zubaydah was first captured.

At the same time, some CIA personnel at Detention Site Green were beginning to object to what they were seeing. Several collectively sent a cable to CIA Headquarters saying that they believed the torture techniques were "approaching the legal limit." The cable drew a swift rebuke from Counterterrorism Center Director Jose Rodriguez.

"Strongly urge that any speculative language as to the legality of given activities or, more precisely, judgment calls as to their legality vis-à-vis operational guidelines for this activity agreed upon and vetted at the most senior levels of the

agency, be refrained from in written traffic (email or cable traffic.) Such language is not helpful."[136]

"Such language" could also create a paper trail that might be subpoenaed at some point in the future, or become the subject of a Freedom of Information Act request.

Rodriguez wanted his Headquarters personnel to understand that what the interrogation team was doing to Abu Zubaydah was legal. Several Headquarters officers planned a visit to Detention Site Green to observe the torture personally. The torture sessions were being taped so that Headquarters officers would be able to watch at their leisure (the tapes were later destroyed on Rodriguez's order). But some officers apparently wished to see the process firsthand. In August 2002, a group of Headquarters officers, including a representative of CTC Legal and the deputy chief of Alec Station, CTC's Osama bin Laden unit, went to Detention Site Green and watched as Abu Zubaydah was tortured, including on the water board.[137]

Satisfied that the interrogation team was doing exactly what it was supposed to, Headquarters ordered that the torture continue. According to Senate investigators, the interrogators were now reporting that during the waterboarding, Abu Zubaydah could become "hysterical" and "distressed to the level that he was unable to effectively communicate." And that the waterboarding "resulted in immediate fluid intake and involuntary leg, chest, and arm spasms" and "hysterical pleas."[138] In one incident, Abu Zubaydah nearly drowned, becoming "completely unresponsive, with bubbles rising through his open, full mouth." He only regained consciousness after the intervention of the medical team.[139]

Despite their rebuke from Rodriguez, many CIA officers at Detention Site Green remained appalled by what they saw.

Senate investigators found that their accounts supported this generalized feeling of concern and disgust.

> *August 5, 2002: "Today's first session...had a profound effect on all staff members present...it seems the collective opinion that we should not go much further...everyone seems strong for now but if the group has to continue... we cannot guarantee how much longer."*

> *August 8, 2002: "Several on the team profoundly affected... some to the point of tears and choking up."*

> *August 9, 2002: "'Two, perhaps three (personnel) likely to elect transfer away' from the detention site if the decision is made to continue with the CIA's enhanced interrogation techniques."*

> *August 11, 2002: "Viewing the pressures on Abu Zubaydah on video 'has produced strong feelings of futility (and legality) of escalating or even maintaining the pressure.' Per viewing the tapes, 'prepare for something not seen previously'."*[140]

In mid-August, the torture stopped almost as quickly as it had started. Detention Site Green personnel offered their conclusion to Headquarters: Abu Zubaydah had been truthful, and he had not had any new terrorist threat information.[141] The torture had produced no actionable intelligence. It had disrupted no new attacks. It certainly had saved no American lives.

The most important intelligence that Abu Zubaydah had revealed came *before* he was tortured—this despite the fact that the number of intelligence reports produced from his interrogation sessions before and during the torture were roughly equal. A CIA after-action report uncovered by Senate investigators noted that, "During the months of August and September 2002, Abu Zubaydah produced 91 intelligence reports, four fewer than the first two months of his CIA detention. CIA records indicate that the type of intelligence Abu Zubaydah provided remained relatively constant prior to and after the use of the CIA's enhanced interrogation techniques. According to CIA records, Abu Zubaydah provided information on 'Al Qaeda activities, plans, capabilities, and relationships,' in addition to information on 'its leadership structure, including personalities, decision-making processes, training, and tactics.'"[142]

Senate investigators also found that "CIA documents identified the 'key intelligence' acquired from Abu Zubaydah as information related to suspected terrorists Jose Padilla and Binyam Mohammad, information on English-speaking Al Qaeda member Jaffar al-Tayyar, and information identifying KSM as the mastermind of the September 11, 2001 attacks, who used the alias 'Mukhtar.' All of this information was acquired by FBI special agents shortly after Abu Zubaydah's capture."[143]

None of it came as a result of the torture techniques.

Cold, hard facts notwithstanding, the CIA told the National Security Council that their torture techniques "were effective and were producing meaningful results."[144] This is almost impossible to credit as true—by any accepted definition of "effective" or "meaningful" or "results." At the same time, Jessen and Mitchell reported to Headquarters that their interrogation program had been a success. They recommended that "the aggressive phase at [Detention Site Green] should be used as a template for future interrogations of high-value captives." This was not because the program had produced useful information, according to Senate investigators, but because "their use confirmed that Abu Zubaydah did not possess the intelligence that CIA Headquarters had assessed Abu Zubaydah to have."[145]

There was no Agency "hot wash"—a meeting of all participants immediately after an operation, where participants discuss what happened, lessons learned, and next steps. There was nothing in CIA cable traffic to indicate widespread regret that a man had been tortured for no apparent reason. There was no acknowledgment—even to the president or the Congressional oversight committees—that a policy of torture had not produced intelligence. Instead, Detention Site Green recommended to Headquarters that psychologists "familiar with interrogation exploitation, and resistance to interrogation"—most likely a reference to Jessen and Mitchell—"should shape compliance of high-value captives prior to debriefing by substantive experts." [146]

At the same time that Detention Site Green was reaching the conclusion that Abu Zubaydah had no actionable intelligence to provide, CTC analysts were writing in the president's Daily Brief (PDB) that Abu Zubaydah was still likely withholding "significant threat information," including information on Al Qaeda operatives in the United States.[147] The PDB article made no mention of the torture techniques, nor did it say that CIA officers in the field believed that Abu Zubaydah was, in fact, cooperating fully and not withholding information.[148]

After his torture had concluded, Abu Zubaydah was moved to a series of secret prisons around the world, the locations of which still remain classified. Then, finally, on September 5, 2006, Abu Zubaydah was transferred into US military custody and sent to the prison at Guantanamo, Cuba. He is still incarcerated there today.

Chapter Ten

Life in Guantanamo

For over four years, Abu Zubaydah had been the subject of inhumane treatment culminating in actual torture while in CIA custody. Unfortunately for him, things did not get markedly better for him when he was sent to Guantanamo. There was more of everything in store—including torture.

On September 6, 2006, Abu Zubaydah and thirteen other men considered "high-value detainees" were sent from a CIA black site to Guantanamo Bay. While their days of torture in CIA custody were over, another round was about to begin. The DoD had its own torture program in place. This program has played out in Afghanistan and in Abu Ghraib, Iraq—but it was created in Guantanamo. The program was a mixture of CIA-approved techniques, along with "tricks" garnered from the North Koreans, the Soviets, and from CIA human experiments like MK-ULTRA.

For Abu Zubaydah, it began even before he landed. During the long flight to Guantanamo, the DoD placed rubber gloves on his hands, earmuffs over his ears, and goggles covered in black paint on his face. The effect produced is called "sensory deprivation." The Soviets had used it effectively against Czechoslovakians in the 1970s. The technique caused subjects to feel panic, confusion, and helplessness—which ultimately led to submission.

Within just a few hours after arriving in Guantanamo, Abu Zubaydah was given a controversial anti-malaria drug called mefloquine. When taken at a dose of 250 milligrams, mefloquine is known to produce harsh side effects such as anxiety, paranoia, hallucinations, aggression, psychotic behavior, mood changes, depression, memory impairment, convulsions, loss of coordination (ataxia), and suicidal ideation. Even though Abu Zubaydah did not have malaria, and there is no malaria in Guantanamo, Abu Zubaydah was given 1,250 milligrams. Mefloquine is a quinolone, part of the family of drugs the CIA had experimented with during MK-ULTRA. Designed and operated by the CIA, the MK-ULTRA project involved illegal drug experimentation on both members of the military and on civilians. One of the goals of MK-ULTRA was to identify drugs that might be useful in interrogation and torture scenarios. According to the CIA's own notes from the project, the use of quinolone drugs in interrogation settings was found to have potential. As the Agency put it: "an adversary service could use such drugs to produce anxiety or terror in medically unsophisticated subjects unable to distinguish drug-induced psychosis from actual insanity."

Major Remington Nevin—an Army public health physician who formerly worked at the Armed Forces Health Surveillance Center and has written extensively about mefloquine—has characterized taking this drug at such a high dosage as" pharmacologic waterboarding."[149] Nevin believes administering the drug at the dosage Abu Zubaydah received involves "unacceptably high risks of potentially severe neuropsychiatric side effects, including seizures, intense vertigo, hallucinations, paranoid delusions, aggression, panic, anxiety, severe insomnia, and thoughts of suicide . . . These side effects could be as severe as those intended through the application of 'enhanced interrogation techniques.'" Mefloquine is a fat-soluble drug. Unlike water soluble drugs, which are designed to stay in a person's system for just a few hours, fat-soluble drugs have a very long half-life. This is important, since a massive dose of mefloquine—such as the one Abu Zubaydah and the other detainees at Guantanamo were given—produces effects that could last for weeks or months.

After being sensory deprived and overdosed with a known hallucinogen, Abu Zubaydah was taken to a top-secret base within Guantanamo known as "Camp Seven" and put into isolation. There he stayed for thirty days. He was not given the right to receive visits from the Red Cross or from a chaplain, which is explicitly called for for prisoners of war by the Geneva Convention. The only human contact he had was with his interrogators. This was intentional, and meant to instill in Abu Zubaydah a sense that they were the only ones upon whom he could depend, and the only ones who might ultimately be his savior.

After thirty days in isolation, Abu Zubaydah was moved to an isolated cell on a cell block in Camp Seven, and given limited recreation time and human contact. His new schedule also involved being taken to frequent interrogations. Interrogations at Guantanamo at the time were conducted using the Biderman Principle.

Albert Biderman was a sociologist who had studied methods employed by the Chinese communists to coerce information and false confessions from American servicemen captured during the Korean War. During that war, many captured US service members confessed to horrific war crimes of which they were innocent while in Chinese custody. The Chinese filmed these confessions and used them in propaganda. Biderman wanted to know what type of interrogation had made the US service members confess like this. After conducting an extensive study, in 1957 Biderman published his findings in the *Bulletin New York Academy of Medicine,* in a piece titled "Communist Attempts to Elicit False Confessions from Air Force Prisoners of War." The article contained a version of the chart reproduced here, illustrating the methods of interrogation, their effects, and variations upon them.

General Method	Effects (Purposes)	Variants
1. Isolation	Deprives victim of all social support of his ability to resist. Develops an intense concern with self. Makes victim dependent upon interrogator.	Complete solitary confinement. Complete isolation. Semi-isolation. Group isolation.
2. Monopolization of Perception	Fixes attention upon immediate predicament. Fosters introspection. Eliminates stimuli competing with those controlled by captor. Frustrates all action not consistent with compliance.	Physical isolation. Darkness or bright light. Barren environment. Restricted movement. Monotonous food.

3. Induced Debilitation and Exhaustion	Weakens mental and physical ability to resist	Semi-starvation. Exposure. Exploitation of wounds. Induced illness. Sleep deprivation. Prolonged constraint. Prolonged interrogation. Forced writing. Over-exertion.
4. Threats	Cultivates anxiety and despair	Threats of death. Threats of non [return?]. Threats of endless interrogation and isolation. Threats against family. Vague threats. Mysterious changes of treatment.
5. Occasional indulgences	Provides positive motivation for compliance. Hinders adjustment to deprivation.	[Occasional?] favors. Fluctuations of interrogator's attitudes. Promises. Rewards for partial compliance. Tantalizing.
6. Demonstrating "Omnipotence" and "Omniscience"	Suggests futility of resistance.	Confrontation. Pretending cooperation taken for granted. Demonstrating complete control over victim's fate.

7. Degradation	Makes cost of resistance more damaging to self-esteem than capitulation. Reduces prisoner to 'animal level' concerns.	Personal hygiene prevented. Filthy infested surrounds. Demeaning punishments. Insults and taunts. Denial of privacy.
8. Enforcing Trivial Demands	Develops habits of compliance.	Forced writing. Enforcement of minute rules.

Biderman found the techniques used by the Chinese to be "abominable and outrageous," adding that "probably no other aspect of communism reveals more thoroughly its disrespect for truth and the individuals than its resort to these techniques."

Even though Biderman detested the techniques and characterized them as torture, the DoD soon made them the centerpiece of its own interrogation program. As time went by, Biederman's work apparently stayed at the fore of the DoD. Copies of Biderman's chart—reproduced word for word—were found hanging on the wall in the Interrogation Control Elements Office at Guantanamo (and on a wall in an office in Abu Ghraib prison in Iraq) during an inquiry of detainee abuse by the Senate Select Committee.

The motto at Guantanamo is "Safe, Humane, Legal, and Transparent." No characterization of what goes on there could be further from the truth. Guantanamo is a place built, inaugurated, and maintained by deception and lies. Hundreds of men accused of being America's enemies during the "Global War on Terror" were tortured and treated inhumanely at Guantanamo. None were given the right of due process, none were charged with a crime, and some died in custody. Many are still there.

To some observers, the hypocrisy and permissiveness on display at Guantanamo is connected to problematic trends running through other parts of American society.

When the housing crisis hit in 2008, politicians and bankers who had clamored for dangerous deregulation were seldom censured and never sent to prison, yet millions of poor and working people lost their homes. When incidences of abuse were brought to light at Guantanamo or Abu Ghraib, the high-ranking officers on the bases and the suits at the Pentagon—who had formulated and greenlit this behavior—were never held to account. Instead, any incidents that got as far as the media were always blamed on the low-ranking privates and sergeants that had been following their so-called "lawful orders."

When innocent, unarmed black men in America are gunned down in the streets by police just for living in the wrong zip code, law enforcement officers are rarely held accountable. Neither are the police chiefs or the politicians who appoint the police chiefs. Instead, the crimes are blamed on the victims themselves. If he was innocent, then what was he doing in that neighborhood? In Guantanamo, when a detainee dies in custody, those charged with holding the inmates and keeping them alive until their status is resolved are never held accountable. Instead, the crime is blamed on the victim. It is, somehow, the detainee's fault for having died. The death is characterized as form of "asymmetrical warfare."

Abu Zubaydah now has spent fifteen years of his life in custody. Conditions have improved slightly at Guantanamo, but that is not saying much. While Abu Zubaydah may not be undergoing a regimen of torture at the moment, he is still in a maximum security prison far from the protections of the mainland. He likely wonders each day if he will ever be freed from the legal black hole in which he finds himself. In a way, not knowing if you will ever see your loved ones again—much less the larger world—has to be a kind of torture in and of itself.

Some of the accusations made against Abu Zubaydah are probably true. Many of the accusations made against him are demonstrably *not* true. But whatever his actual transgressions, a strong case can be made that he has now paid for them many times over. During the last fifteen years, he has withstood unimaginable torture, confinement, and cruel and inhumane treatment. He still has not been charged with any crime and has been denied due process. Abu Zubaydah needs something that is becoming rarer than it should be in a nation that was founded on the Rule of Law.

Abu Zubaydah needs a fair trial.

Failure to give him that is tantamount to failing to adhere to the basic precepts upon which our nation was founded. George Washington spoke out explicitly against the mistreatment or torture of prisoners of war on numerous occasions—including in his charge to the Northern Expeditionary Force on September 14, 1775, and in his famous missive following the Battle of Trenton on December 26, 1776. Even President Trump—who has stated that he believes torture "works"—has said that his anti-torture Secretary of Defense James Mattis will have the power to "override" him on the issue.

America is at a crossroads. We can build on our fundamental values. We can admit what was done, admit that it was wrong—a horrible misstep at the very least—and resolve to do better, to *be* better, in the future. Or we can fail to learn from the evidence showing torture is neither useful or effective, and do nothing.

But if we are to remain the acknowledged leaders of the free world—the beacon of light and hope and justice that the United States of America has always been—then we must come to terms with what has happened. We must make it right again. We must pledge ourselves anew to the rule of law.

And we must, above all, see that this man has justice.

ENDNOTES

1   Abu Zubaydah Diaries, Volume 4, page 21.
2   Ibid, page 21-22.
3   Ibid, page 22.
4   Ibid.
5   *The Reluctant Spy: My Secret Life in the CIA's War on Terror*, by John Kiriakou with Michael Ruby, Bantam Books, New York, 2010, page xiv.
6   Ibid, page xv.
7   Ibid, page 111-112.
8   Ibid, page xv.
9   Ibid, page 109.
10 Ibid, page xvi.
11 Ibid, page 110.
12 Ibid, page 110-111.
13 Ibid, page 111.
14 Ibid.
15 Ibid, page xvii.
16 Ibid.
17 Ibid.

18 Abu Zubaydah Diaries, Volume 4, page 25.

19 The Reluctant Spy, page 112.

20 Ibid.

21 Ibid, page xviii.

22 Ibid.

23 Ibid, pages xviii-xix.

24 Ibid, page xix.

25 Ibid, page 113.

26 Ibid.

27 Ibid.

28 Ibid, page 113.

29 Ibid, page 114.

30 Ibid.

31 Ibid, page 115.

32 Ibid.

33 Ibid, page 116.

34 Ibid, page 117.

35 Ibid.

36 Ibid.

37 Ibid, page 118.

38 Ibid.

39 Ibid, pages 118-119.

40 Ibid, page 119.

41 Ibid.

42 Ibid.

43 Ibid, page 120.

44 Ibid.

45 "Wanted Spies Who Speak Arabic" By Michael Moran Aug. 26, 2003 HYPERLINK "http://www.nbcnews.com/id/3071401/ns/us_news-only/t/wanted-spies-who-speak-arabic/" \l ".WNqMUVUrKUl" http://www.nbcnews.com/id/3071401/ns/us_news-only/t/wanted-spies-who-speak-arabic/#.WNqMUVUrKUl

46 Verbatim Transcript of Combatant Status Review Tribunal for ISN 10024 (KSM) http://i.a.cnn.net/cnn/2007/images/03/14/transcript_ISN10024.pdf

47 Abu Zubaydah's Diary Volume 1 http://america.aljazeera. com/multimedia/2013/11/original-documentabuzubayd- ahdiariesvolumeone.html

48 Zayn Abu Zubaydah temporarily inherited leadership of the House of Martyrs on or about September 15, 1994, "until the person in charge comes back from his marriage vacation… or…." Zayn Abu Zubaydah became the leader of the House of Martyrs when he noted in his diary, "Be- cause of some certain circumstances I decided to stay in Peshawar as the person in charge of the Martyr's House." See Zayn Abu Zubaydah, The Diary of Abu Zubaydah, Vol- ume IV, p. 26, available at: http://america.aljazeera.com/ multimedia/2013/11/original-documentabuAbu Zubayd- ahdiariesvolumefour.html.; Zayn Abu Zubaydah, The Diary of Abu Zubaydah, Volume IV, p. 30, available at: http:// america.aljazeera.com/multimedia/2013/11/original-docu- mentabuAbu Zubaydahdiariesvolumefour.html.

49 Translation done by Seton Hall University School of Law's Senior Research Fellow Ghalib Mahmoud.

50 Ibid.

51 Ibid.

52 Based on thesis written by Dustin Joseph Lask.

53 Report written for the Combating Terrorism Center at West Point by US Navy Lieutenant Commander Youssef Aboul-Enein, titled "Radical Theories on Defending Mus- lim Land through Jihad."

54 Ibid.

55 Photo taken of Sayyaf and other Afghan warlords in the White House with President Reagan.

56 Document obtained at Combating Terrorism Center at West Point.

57 There is no direct evidence that the planned attacks on Jordan were planned by the same group that planned the at- tacks at LAX.

58 All details I have about the CIA reports were revealed to me by a source who wants to stay anonymous; however, it was

verified in an interview I conducted with Ali-Saufan on October 18, 2012

59 Library of Congress Report May 2002, "A Global Overview Of Narcotics-Funded Terrorist And Other Extremist Groups" prepared by the Federal Research Division, Library of Congress, under an Interagency Agreement with the Department of Defense.

60 FBI Memo dated 12/29/1999, addressed to all field offices, from FBI Counterterrorism Division.

61 Omar Abdel Rahman lived in New York, but often would visit Hisham Diab in California, and attend his meeting in his home.

62 United States House of Representatives Judiciary Subcommittee on Immigration and Claims, report dated January 25, 2000, titled "International Terrorism and Immigration Policy."

63 Khalil Al-Deek's whereabouts now unknown. Some speculate he was killed in Pakistan in 2005.

64 United States vs. Abdurahman Alamoudi case no. 03-1009M.

65 There are currently as many as 36,000 Palestinian refugees with ancestral ties to Yabna.

66 Al Zawahiri was born June 19, 1951. It is widely reported that 1979, Al Zawahiri had gone to Afghanistan to resist the Soviet Union's occupation. It was there he met Osama bin Laden, the head of Al-Qaeda. After returning to Egypt from Afghanistan in 1981 Al Zawahiri joined the Egyptian Islamic Jihad (EIJ), and officially became its leader in 1993. The EIJ merged with Al-Qaeda in 1998, issuing a joint statement with bin Laden. Following the September 11, 2001, terrorist attacks in the United States, Al Zawahiri appeared on the FBI's Most Wanted Terrorists list. His whereabouts remain unknown, although he is believed to be in tribal Pakistan where he regularly releases videos and statements. Since Bin Laden's Death Al Zawahiri has taken over as the leader of Al-Qaeda.

67 El-Dahab was an Egyptian medical student who moved to California at the request of Ali Mohamed. El-Dahab acted as a telephone operator for the Islamic Jihad network, distributed forged documents, learned how to fly gliders and

helicopters, and recruited additional US sleeper agents. El-Dahab moved to Egypt in 1998, was arrested, and confessed his role in an Egyptian trial in 1999.

68 *Triple Cross Bin Laden's Spy In America (Full Documentary)*, You Tube (Jan. 10, 2014), https://www.youtube.com/watch?v=ktLEYPUWOOw.

69 Ibid

70 Ibid

71 Wright, Lawrence. *Looming Tower* (First Vintage Books, Random House, 2007), 180. Mohamed was described as tall, in shape, and spoke four languages: French, Hebrew, English, and Arabic.

72 Special operations force that handles unconventional warfare, foreign internal defense, special reconnaissance, direct action, and counterterrorism.

73 *Triple Cross Bin Laden's Spy In America (Full Documentary)*, You Tube (Jan. 10, 2014), https://www.youtube.com/watch?v=ktLEYPUWOOw.

74 Ibid. The new Egyptian military was targeting and dismissing Muslim extremists. This occurred in 1984. Ali Mohammed became outspoken about the issue.

75 Wright, Lawrence. *Looming Tower* (First Vintage Books, Random House, 2007), 180.

76 Hays, Tom, *Egyptian agent worked with Green Berets, bin Laden*, Jerusalem Post, December 31, 2001.

77 *Triple Cross Bin Laden's Spy In America (Full Documentary)*, You Tube (Jan. 10, 2014), https://www.youtube.com/watch?v=ktLEYPUWOOw.

78 Ibid.

79 Ibid.

80 Ibid.

81 Ibid.

82 Ibid.

83 Ibid.

84 Ibid.

85 Ibid.

86 Ibid.

87 *USA v. Mohamed* http://cryptome.org/usa-v-mohamed.htm

88 *Triple Cross Bin Laden's Spy In America (Full Documentary)*, You Tube (Jan. 10, 2014), https://www.youtube.com/watch?v=ktLEYPUWOOw.

89 Ibid.

90 US Senate Select Committee on Intelligence, "The Torture Report," 2014, page 18.

91 Ibid, page 19.

92 Ibid.

93 Ibid, page 19.

94 Ibid, page 20.

95 Ibid.

96 CIA Inspector General Special Review, "Counterterrorism Detention and Interrogation Activities (September 2001 – October 2003), May 7, 2004. http://nsarchive.gwu.edu/torture_archive/20040507.pdf, retrieved December 30, 2015.

97 US Senate Select Committee on Intelligence, "The Torture Report," 2014, page 21.

98 Leopold, Jason, "Cheney Admits he 'Signed Off' on Waterboarding of Three Guantanamo Prisoners," Atlantic Free Press, December 29, 2008.

99 Warrick, Joby. "Top Officials Knew in 2002 of Harsh Interrogations," *Washington Post,* http://www.washingtonpost.com/wp-dyn/content/article/2008/09/24/AR2008092403355.html, retrieved January 5, 2016.

100 US Code, Title 18, Part I, Chapter 113C, § 2340A - Torture. https://www.law.cornell.edu/uscode/text/18/2340A, retrieved December 30, 2015.

101 "UN Convention Against Torture and Other Cruel, Inhuman or Degrading Treatment or Punishment," http://www.hrweb.org/legal/cat.html. Retrieved December 30, 2015.

102 http://www.npr.org/2007/11/03/15886834/waterboarding-a-tortured-history

103 Testimony of Ali Soufan, United States Senate Committee on the Judiciary, May 13, 2009.

104 Ibid.

105 US Senate Select Committee on Intelligence, "The Torture Report," 2014, page 25.

106 Ibid.

107 Testimony of Ali Soufan, United States Senate Committee on the Judiciary, May 13, 2009.

108 Ibid.

109 Ibid.

110 US Senate Select Committee on Intelligence, "The Torture Report," 2014, page 25.

111 Testimony of Ali Soufan, United States Senate Committee on the Judiciary, May 13, 2009.

112 US Senate Select Committee on Intelligence, "The Torture Report," 2014, page 33.

113 Ibid

114 Ibid.

115 Letter from Deputy Assistant Attorney General John Yoo to CIA Acting General Counsel John Rizzo, July 19, 2002.

116 US Senate Select Committee on Intelligence, "The Torture Report," 2014, page 34.

117 Warrick, Joby. "Top Officials Knew in 2002 of Harsh Interrogations," *Washington Post*, http://www.washingtonpost.com/wp-dyn/content/article/2008/09/24/AR2008092403355.html, Retrieved January 5, 2016.

118 US Senate Select Committee on Intelligence, "The Torture Report," 2014, pages 34-35.

119 US Senate Select Committee on Intelligence, "The Torture Report," 2014, page 35.

120 Ibid, page 36.

121 Ibid, page 37.

122 Ibid, page 37.

123 Ibid.

124 Ibid, page 38. Senate investigators found that Secretary of State Colin Powell and Secretary of Defense Donald Rumsfeld were not briefed on the torture program. Similarly, the Chairmen, Vice Chairmen, and members of the Senate Select Committee on Intelligence and the House Permanent Select Committee on Intelligence were kept in the dark.

125 US Senate Select Committee on Intelligence, "The Torture Report," 2014, page 38.
126 Ibid page 39.
127 Ibid, page 40.
128 Ibid.
129 Ibid, pages 40-41.
130 Ibid, page 41.
131 Ibid.
132 Ibid, page 41, footnote 188.
133 Ibid, page 41-42.
134 Ibid, page 42.
135 Ibid.
136 Ibid, page 43.
137 Ibid.
138 Ibid.
139 Ibid.
140 Ibid, pages 44-45.
141 Ibid, page 45.
142 Ibid, page 45, footnote 215.
143 Ibid, page 47.
144 Ibid, page 45.
145 Ibid, page 46.
146 Ibid.
147 Ibid, page 47.
148 Ibid, page 46.
149 EXCLUSIVE: Controversial Drug Given to All Guantanamo Detainees Akin to "Pharmacologic Waterboarding" by Jason Leopold and Jeffrey Kaye, http://www.truth-out.org/news/item/253:exclusive-controversial-drug-given-to-all-guanta-namo-detainees-akin-to-pharmacologic-waterboarding